FINDING DIAMONDS

12 inspiring women who dig deep and share their story to TRANSFORM YOUR life and create new legacies

ALYSSA ANN MERRITT

Copyright © 2021 Alyssa Ann Merritt

FINDING DIAMONDS

All rights reserved. No part of this publication may be reproduced, distributed, or transmitted in any form or by any means, including photocopying, recording, or other electronic or mechanical methods, without the prior written permission of the publisher, except in the case of brief quotations embodied in critical reviews and certain other noncommercial uses permitted by copyright law. For permission requests, write to the publisher, addressed "Attention: Permissions Coordinator," at info@beyondpublishing.net

Quantity sales special discounts are available on quantity purchases by corporations, associations, and others. For details, contact the publisher at the address above.

Orders by U.S. trade bookstores and wholesalers. Email info@BeyondPublishing.net

The Beyond Publishing Speakers Bureau can bring authors to your live event. For more information or to book an event contact the Beyond Publishing Speakers Bureau speak@BeyondPublishing.net

The Author can be reached directly at BeyondPublishing.net

Manufactured and printed in the United States of America distributed globally by BeyondPublishing.net

New York | Los Angeles | London | Sydney

ISBN Hardcover: 978-1-637920-30-5

ISBN Softcover: 978-1-637920-13-8

I am so grateful for God, the love of Jesus, and the living Holy Spirit. I am grateful for my husband, Michael, my daughters, Annalise and Sarah, and my dad, Charles who inspire and believe in me.

I love you.

This book is dedicated

To every person of any age who is looking for hope and tired of living in fear. Someone looking for joy.

To our loved ones in heaven, we miss you and we look forward to the day we meet again, all fur babies included.

A special thank you to my bonus son, Jacob, my brother, and my sister. You helped me make it this far.

A heartfelt thank you to each Woman who believed in this project to create change in the hearts of all beings all over the World for God's glory. The encouragement and support each family gave to one another during this process was simply amazing.

Looking for what's new is 2021?

It's the number five, directly linked to God's grace, mercy, and favor. Grace: an unmerited favor that comes as a result of God's love. The people in the world are going to rise up in faith over the fear of the worldly things, and God is going to give us grace for our sins and bless our hearts with peace, and all the people of the world will say, "Amen". Let's get our priorities straight.

I am not just talking to the believer.

What's the most prevalent thing in today's world? Fear.

What is the remedy to fear? FAITH.

Faith over fear is what humbled these 12 women to be obedient to God's words placed on their heart when I asked them to be a coauthor. What a blessing and lesson this book has been. March of this year, I stepped out of fear and into my faith. Fear had no more control of my life. Every day has not been an easy day, but every day has been rewarding. My word for 2020 was Courage, and that is exactly what God gave me. To feel the fear and do it anyway is Courage. This book took courage. Each story took courage to tell.

Each woman tells a story of a time in their life when they could not find the next step, and like me, faith was their only option. When we did not understand, I can't say enough, we leaned into God and trusted His words that we were desperately holding onto. Every woman has a different experience and lesson, which is just more proof that no matter your path, you can start anew and find the right path. Find the inspiration in the words of these true stories as their love and hearts pour into yours, giving you hope.

I can't do enough justice to introduce each author. You will meet them through the eyes of their stories and their spirit of hope to make a difference in your life.

These 12 women who were mostly strangers crossed my path through prayer and obedience. No one knew the others' stories but everyone had the same objective which was showing their faith in God and giving Him glory in hopes to inspire others.

I pray you feel the spirit of God move within you while you read these stories and be open to non-judgement, but empathy and appreciation for each one's humbleness.

Dear Lord,

Bless each child, girl, teen, woman, or other person reading this book to hear your love through our words, as we know words are important to our own mindset. Help each story give hope to anyone who is struggling and has lost sight. We know everyone is special to you and everyone was born with a purpose. Help us to build a tribe for you, Lord, to change the lives of all our loved ones and all others who cross our path. Let us be your light, Lord, and your salt to the earth. Let each one reading this book, Lord, aspire to be a role model and an influencer of the right words. Let each of us feel your love while we try to find the love for ourselves. We understand things may be challenging at times, but we choose to believe in our hearts, minds, and souls that you are with us every step of the way, Lord, and you will triumph over all. You are the beginning and the end, Father. Help us to stay obedient in your word for the world's change of heart. Set our minds free of fear, Lord, and set our minds at peace.

In Jesus's name, we are forever grateful.

Amen

TABLE OF CONTENTS

CHAPTER 1: *Kingdom Mindset* 9

CHAPTER 2: *Finding Peace* 19

CHAPTER 3: *Tears that Heal* 27

CHAPTER 4: *Victory* 37

CHAPTER 5: *Resilience Out of Rejection* 45

CHAPTER 6: *Finding the Root* 53

CHAPTER 7: *Robe of Strength* 61

CHAPTER 8: *Diamond Season* 69

CHAPTER 9: *Overcoming Darkness* 75

CHAPTER 10: *To God Be The Glory* 83

CHAPTER 11: *From God's Grace to God's Mercy* 91

CHAPTER 12: *Finding Freedom* 101

CHAPTER 1

KINGDOM MINDSET

ALYSSA ANN JERGER MERRITT

It was 1985 and I just turned 14 when I was on a family vacation and I began the early stages of my near-death experience. As we made an emergency flight home and by the time the plane landed, I could barely walk. I needed assistance up the ramp to a wheelchair. I went to my pediatrician, who sent me home with "flu-like symptoms" and by that evening, I could not walk without help. The next day, I was completely paralyzed, except on one side of my face. No one knew what was wrong, I could not be diagnosed or get the rapid onset to cease. Guillain-Barré syndrome, a rapid onset of muscle weakness caused by the immune system damaging the peripheral nervous system, and was not a very well-known disease in 1985. During the acute phase, the disorder can be life-threatening, and it was. I know everyone was praying. I knew everyone was in the best hands. The biggest problem to me at the time was the doctors and nurses not really knowing about the disease. It was a scary time.

In the ICU department, I had the talk with the family pastor on faith and asked Jesus into my heart so I was saved. I also asked the hard question, "Am I going to make it?" and I heard the answer, "We are trying". I was at a point in my young life where I was told there was only one more thing to try, and the answer came only by divine intervention as one doctor overheard my physicians talking as they passed in the hallway.

As I got older, God started revealing more as I recognize having PTSD from the experience I never processed. This awareness was the beginning of a beautiful, faithful relationship and a better understanding of myself. To think, it all started with a little tingling in my hands and feet. It is crazy to think here I am 36 years later as proof that "I can do all things through Christ who strengthens me" Philippians 4:13 You hold the same value.

My parents divorced when I was 7. I lived with my dad, which included having an estimated 100 people in my immediate family that made up my influencers and role models. Plus add on friends and all the people my grandmother took on from the section 8 housing where she lived and where I spent a lot of time growing up. I lived my own soap opera with every type of life situation from easy to unbelievable touching my life in one way or another. I knew too much of other people's business from spending time at my Mema's. All of these experiences were embedded in my mind for years and gave me several things like trust issues, boundary issues, pain, empathy, love, understanding, and prayer. The bigger picture of it all has brought me this far in life. I am a survivor in spite of it all. When we change our thought and focus, we change our habits and words then our life changes. All of our personal life circumstances, situations, experiences, and pain are between you and God. Although there is a lot of judgement; we are not here for judgement. I have lived my own life of foolishness and pain. I had moments when I did not have God in my forethought. I learned better. You can too.

No matter what struggles I have been through in the past, I know now I am no longer in that bear trap. I am in a place where God is fulfilling a promise, He placed on my heart 27 years ago to write this book for you. God has placed the right people in my life up to this point to fulfill that promise, no matter how good or bad. I had to be obedient when they showed up to take action, get uncomfortable, and work through the process to follow my heart. How do I know today I am on the path, you might ask? I know because I am taking the actions to have a mature relationship with God by knowing his word from the Bible. I believe the words He says, and I use them as an armor every day to fight off negative talk, to give encouragement to others, to love my neighbor, and love myself.

God is faithful, pouring blessing into my life, and even though I forgot HIM many times during the years, the seeds were planted as a little girl and watered sporadically throughout my life. I always give thanks to God for His grace and mercy while I was learning. It is how I made it to write this chapter. There is meaning to everyone's life. My near-death experience put me in touch with "another level of awareness" as some say. I knew who I had to count on and always tried to love like Jesus, yet I would not remember HIM in EVERY decision I made throughout life. I found not knowing the true living Holy Spirit blocks the blessing of contentment and complete joy.

Everyone has encountered different mindsets and experiences that effect their current mindset and decisions. This is why we *must* set our mind on God and Godly things, like basic humanity, love, kindness, patience, empathy, trust, honesty, and the other fruits of the Spirit. "Do unto others as you would want done to you," as the Bible says.

When we you don't start out in the right mindset or don't live with integrity, a foothold is taken in our mind and soul. We must stay intentional with our thoughts and minds, because there is a spiritual warfare happening. There are some breaking of generational bondage and new legacies coming right out of this book, in Jesus's name. You are not reading this on accident or by any coincidence. Make a wise choice for yourself today and accept the love of Jesus Christ, our savior.

When I decided to become a life coach, I realized all my life was perfect preparation. See, God has a bigger plan. Our job is to stay obedient and lean on him, not our own understandings. Know that you are loved and here on purpose. Honestly, we are our own worst enemies. It's not what happens to us; it's how we handle the situation and our reactions. Don't take on other people's problems. I have struggled with this through life and learned to love in relationships with people as they find their own walk with God. I loved the unlovable acts, including myself at times.

So, what does a warrior do? They put on armor, and that is why every day, you put on the whole armor of God, "that ye may be able to stand against the wiles of the devil", as it states in Ephesians 6. The armor of God is the belt of truth, breastplate of righteousness, shoes with the preparation of the gospel of peace, shield of faith, helmet of salvation, and the sword of the Spirit (the word of God). You have to make the choice for change in your life and for your future, no matter your past.

My purpose is breaking the straps of generational bondage. We all have a past. I didn't fully understand the depth of generational bondage until much later in life. My parents had little boundaries with me. I was included in conversations that no child understands. I love my parents and my family, so don't misjudge anything I say. When I read the book, *Boundaries with Kids*, by Cloud and Townsend, my life made more sense. The book hit me so hard it was like a car accident. BAM! The authors say, "Adults with boundary problems did not start as a grown-up." The problems come from starting out with no boundaries in childhood.

Having no boundaries can be a learned behavior that carries on into adulthood, thus, you have your generational sins beginning to repeat themselves.

The book states, "Boundaries are the inability to say no to hurtful people and set limits on hurtful behavior from others. The inability to say no to their own destructive impulses. Inability to hear no from others and respect their limits. Inability to delay gratification and accomplish goals and tasks. The tendency to be attracted to irresponsible or hurtful people and then try to 'fix' them. The ability to be easily manipulated or controlled. Inability to confront others and resolve conflicts productively. Experience life as a victim, instead of living it purposefully with a feeling of self-control. Having addictions and compulsions and disorganization and lack of follow-through." Most parents are well-intentioned, but many times, we have no clue there is a boundary problem. If it is still occurring in our life as adults with our parents, then the cycle continues and we pass the limited boundary functioning to our children by foolishness of not knowing better or different. I could stop here, and my life would make sense.

False Evidence Appearing Real: FEAR, it's real

Fear keeps you from your identity and purpose in the world. The problem is if you don't take the time to know God's Holy Spirit and put Him truly first in front of all your fears, you are not going to understand your purpose to its full extent. You are always wanting more, going more, the possibility to stop learning, and get stuck. Life can be overwhelming when you're going about it all the wrong way. You make things harder and bring on your own problems. It's when you STOP and take a minute to visualize and prioritize what's right in life that you then take the steps in the direction where you can escape the madness. You begin to act in courageous ways to further yourself as a person in God's name, because He is the one you count on to persevere. You count on faith in God's Grace to get you through the consequences of something you did or something that might have been out of your control because you did not fully understand or cannot see the whole picture. Living with God's Holy Spirit creates an electricity inside of you to shine, and you are contagious.

I believe everything happens for a reason and everyone we meet is a blessing or a lesson, just like we are for them. Are you a blessing or a lesson? I also believe we make wrong choices thinking they are right mostly because we are foolish by not being mature in our relationship with God. All of these beliefs, I believe, came over time of praying, surviving episodes, and following my righteous path. You see, I have a blessing on my life. You have a blessing on your life. You have to be willing to step into faith and get to know God by reading the Bible, praying, worshiping, and listening for the Lord to show you his way for your life. He has big things in store for all of us and each of us has a purpose. Be the person who can create change in the world by giving hope to everyone that has gone or is going through similar situations. I am your hope. I have lived through some trying times, and I am still here stronger than ever.

Faith and Courage… to have fear and do it anyway

I've learned how to find the blessing in every situation. I can look back on my life and thank God He was with me along the way, even when I endured the most tragedies. I often caused these tragic moments by living in fear and not my faith.

I needed the power of the Holy Spirit to become alive in me to awaken my sleeping spirit hiding from the world caused by hurt and pain. I had to step into my faith and step into my new self. No negotiations! I had some work to do. Do you? It's possible. I heard a man say once, "If there was no such thing as change, there would be no butterflies". How true is that? You must come out of your cocoon and let God show you your true colors and shine like the diamond you are.

Showing someone who feels unlovable the love of Jesus is the best feeling in the world. There is no powerhouse that can outshine the light inside of you.

Mark 5:25 says, "She suffered a great deal under the care of many doctors and had spent all she had, yet instead of getting better, she grew worse. When she heard about Jesus, she came up behind him and the crowd and touched his cloak, because she thought, 'If I just touch his clothes, I will be healed.' Immediately, her bleeding stopped, and she felt in her body that she was freed from her suffering. He found the woman and said, '**Daughter**, your faith has healed you. Go in peace and be freed from your suffering.'" This WAS me.

I was on fire when I had the opportunity to create a new life for myself and began to feel valued again. I faced some fears I had in my heart, mind, and soul. At times, it was as if fear was winning over my faith. Listen, I have faced many lions' dens and Goliaths in life. I am here because I have God on my side. I am accomplishing my dreams because I have the Holy Spirit living in me and through me.

The key to Life Transformation is to start listening to what you are inputting into your mind via books, word of mouth, television, radio, media or phone. Be mindful. I started changing my words, actions, and mindset. I started to remember all the things I once knew but understood today, they applied to ME TOO.

Once you can let go of your past experiences and forgive yourself, you can start in a new direction, believing your purpose, and your value. I am not perfect and still have my "things" I work on. I understand how to love like Jesus in a way I never knew before. I have been fortunate not to let anger and resentment overshadow all my life. This is what I am telling you: fear is real, but it does not have to control your life. You can have faith over fear knowing sometimes things happen that don't make sense, but it's not to make us fearful; that is when you have faith, because you never really know what is around the corner. The pandemic should have taught you this.

I became faithful and obedient, and God put the right people in my path.

There is just a bigger picture and like I did, you may be living with limited beliefs and limited thinking. You may be still listening to the voices inside your head that tell you that you can't or not you. That is simply not true, and I am proof. All you have to do is trust and have faith. I want you to know that no matter what is in your past; it is in your past. You really can't change it or go back and do anything about it. You have to forgive yourself or others if it was harmful, maybe ask forgiveness of others, and do life differently. People will try to keep you in the box because it makes them more comfortable. God gave you a vision for your purpose. Others may not understand and that is ok. Keep moving forward.

What I want you to take away from this is: no matter what life throws at you and no matter where you are, you can make a change in your life TODAY. I decided I was not going to let someone else feel lost, alone, or hopeless if I could help with my story. I've endured mental and physical abuse by myself and others. I am victorious! I pray this helps you to see when you are living the righteous life, God will put the people in your path to make your dreams come true and will fulfill your purpose, just like he did mine. God bless you!

I want to take the time to tell you it's a simple change of life. Use these words; Dear Jesus, please come into my heart and help me to live and love like you. In Jesus's name, amen. Repent your sins, and start reading your bible 20 minutes every day. Listen to transformational pastors, influencers, podcasts, and YouTube. I was once asked what was missing from top motivational speakers, and my answer was "God". He should be the start of everything you do. He is your foundation.

As my mom would say, "This, too, shall pass".

I am Alyssa (A LEE sa) Ann Jerger Merritt. I am here to put a new lease on your life. Spiritual transformation is for eternity. I am a Texan. I have been a life coach for over 20 years. I am a disciple who is here to help others struggling in life and looking for the answer to life. I have struggled with mental health issues and many other life issues. I have empathy. I am married. I am a mother of two beautiful and brilliant daughters, Annalise and Sarah and a bonus son, Jacob, who has accomplished a Master's in psychology. I am a speaker and podcaster. The show is called "Born to Succeed with Michael and Alyssa Merritt". Check it out. I am also a coauthor in the #1 International Best-Selling book called *1Habit to Thrive in a Post-Covid World*. I suggest the book for your library.

Reach out. Never get comfortable with being in an uncomfortable situation. **Never lose hope.** Never feel alone because we are here.

merrittcoachinggroup@gmail.com

Facebook.com/alyssajerger

FB: Merritt Coaching Group (A daily dose of Motivation, Inspiration, Faith, Hope and Love) Richardson, Texas,

FB: Building the Tribe (a Women's group of encouragement)

CHAPTER 2

FINDING PEACE

BRENDA ZIMMERMANN

Finding peace, having good health and happiness is something we all desire in our life. Jeremiah 29:11 "For I know the plans I have for you", says the Lord. They're plans to prosper {good}, and not to harm, but to give you hope and a future. When we're young, we dream of growing up, graduating high school, college, having a high paying job with great benefits, getting married, having a house with the white picket fence. Eventually we have children because that's what everyone does, right? What if the person you choose to do life with doesn't like kids and even hated himself as a kid? He would joke about it but deep down but he was serious. I, on the other hand, have always loved kids, wanted 3, and was blessed with 4 amazing children!

I grew up in a small town in upstate New York. I had an awesome mom and dad, Martha and Billy. Both worked to provide a good life for us. I was also blessed with two really cool brothers, John and Ernie. I was the oldest, but still daddy's little girl! Our parents taught us to stick together and have each other's back. We loved to wrestle, ride bikes, target practice with guns and bow and arrows, fishing at our local lake and river. We would ride motorcycles, four wheelers, and jet skis. In the winter we would ride snowmobiles, go sledding and ice skating. I played basketball, volleyball and softball in jr. high. I played field hockey, was a basketball cheerleader and played softball in high school. Jr high and High school can be a very confusing time in one's life, so being involved in sports provides structure and distractions.

In elementary and Jr high, I spent a lot of weekends at my grandparents' house in the country. I loved being outside, running in the woods, climbing trees, picking blackberries and wild flowers. It was very peaceful. I loved the one-on-one time with my grandma. She was pretty much bed/couch ridden as she suffered from severe rheumatoid arthritis and emphysema. She had smoked cigarettes for most of her life, so there were times she would just gasp for her next breath. I unknowingly contributed to this as I thought it was fun to help her roll her own cigarettes. We'd watch cartoons while doing crafts on Saturday mornings and watch Oral Roberts ministry on Sunday mornings. As a kid, I was confused on why she would pray to God to take her, as my grandpa Bucky was the best at meeting her needs. One day, my mom showed up at Jr high to pick me up in street clothes, she normally was dressed nice as she worked in an office. I learned that my grandma had passed away in her sleep. She was finally resting in peace. She was no longer suffering. My world however was totally turned upside down. Proverbs 3:5-6 "Trust in the Lord with all your heart and lean not in your own understanding; in all your ways acknowledge Him and He will make your paths straight".

Another bump in the road in Jr high was my parents separating. My mom was in an upstairs apartment, while my dad was in a downstairs one. My dad worked in construction as a laborer and also as a longshoreman. Unfortunately, that meant stopping off for beverages with the guys after. My mom had to deal with the 3 of us and work. I remember getting off the bus at school in the morning and just crying. Was I the only kid going through their parents separating or divorcing? I had no peace, what was going to happen to me and my brothers? What would people think? I was also having negative thoughts about my weight, as a parent of a friend would jokingly make snide comments, unfortunately that planted a seed for weight issues in high school. With both parents working a lot, they were not able to attend mine or my brother's athletic events. It was hard not having their support or cheering us on during games. My parents eventually got their act together and reunited. It was still very different but they made it work. We didn't attend church as a family, which I truly believe this was a contributing factor for ongoing strife. Mom was raised Methodist; dad was raised Catholic. There were a lot of issues with family illness, death, etc. that molded my parents and the way they raised us. I talked A LOT in Jr high. Seemed I was always being moved from the back to the front to the office. My punishment was afternoon announcements. Really? More talking!!!

I moved on to High school where I still talked too much! Principal said, "We heard you were coming". I needed to put my energy towards something, so I played Varsity girls field hockey and loved it. Next up was basketball cheerleading, something totally new for me as I wasn't the girly girl type. Doing this forced me to give up my figure skating as practices and games clashed. This truly ended up being right up my alley though. I get to talk to fans {fellow classmates}, cheer and run around like crazy. A negative thought was the way my cheerleading skirt fit. It was a little snug so it caused me to think more about my body image while comparing myself to others. In the spring I played JV softball and got moved up to Varsity. I had played baseball growing up so was I pretty good. I loved third base, the hot spot. Sports in an escape from everything else going on around you. I was good till my Jr year. I had a coach/teacher that jokingly commented on my weight. That combined with previous thoughts and comments sent me into a downward spiral. I literally became anorexic. I could control how much food {caloric intake} and exercising {burning calories} to lose weight. As I looked in the mirror I wanted to lose more, yet to others I was fading away. I did not have comfort & peace with the way I looked.

A friend that I had not seen in a while asked if I was sick or had been in the hospital? No, why? She said I looked ill and was way too thin? That was an eye opener for me. My senior year I needed to get it together. What was I going to do with the rest of my life? A school counselor recommended that I attend BOCES, a trade school. I chose DA= Dental assisting, as it was a half day program while continuing the other half at school to finish requirements for graduation. I ended up becoming treasurer of the class for HOSA [Health occupation Students of America]. I was eager to learn everything I could about dentally assisting. I placed 1st in NYS competition in the Adirondacks, then onto San Antonio Tx for nationals. I placed 5th in the US and that was still not good enough for me. I wanted to be #1. I was hired by Fulton Dental Health Center after my internship. As with DA school, here I was eager to learn everything possible. I was the one who wanted to work with all the dental specialists, even though they could be demanding and difficult at times. I worked with 2 different Endodontist {root canal}, an Orthodontist{braces}, an Oral Surgeon{extraction}, and all general dentists at the practice. It was a great learning experience, but I needed and wanted more. I went onto dental hygiene school in Syracuse, NY. I graduated with honors from the program and moved to Burleson, Texas in June of "87.

My beautiful daughter Brittany arrived October 1st. I stayed home briefly with her and had an itching to start practicing Dental hygiene. I worked in Arlington, Tx. It was quite the change from a small-town upstate NY. I really started to thrive in the practice. I decided to move from country town to city. Britts dad was an Electrical Engineer so he'd work till the job was done and onto the next challenge. I stayed put in Texas and he left to his next assignment. I unfortunately realized we were two different people in two different places in our lives, but Britt was our #1 priority. I did meet an amazing guy Rich, and we had everything in common. We were planning an amazing future, blending our son and daughter as a family when he was tragically killed in a car accident the day, he was to fly to NY to meet my family. Once again, I have suffered an unbelievable loss. The couple that had been watching Brittany while I worked, had been asking me to go to church with them. They saw the pain I was experiencing, so I reluctantly agreed to go. From the moment I walked into the church, I had a calm feeling as if the pastor was speaking directly to me. Then, the tears began to flow from my eyes, my heart was racing as if it was going to beat right out of my chest. I had NEVER EXPERIENCED anything like that in my life. Deb explained that it was the Holy spirit moving in me. We have to grow strong in our weakness. The shepherd will leave the 99 to find that one lost sheep! God will never give up on us. Psalm 16:8 "I know the Lord is always with me. I will not be shaken, for He is right beside me". God knows what you have been through, He will never leave you. I truly believe that from the bottom of my heart.

I eventually met a guy named Jack. He was a true salesman and played a lot of golf. That was a major issue down the road. He traveled with work and was on the road a lot. He always seems to make time for golf. He never wanted kids but I came with one so we made it work. We bought a nice home in Bedford, Tx. After a couple years we had our first daughter, Leesa. She is Miss Personality, full of life, our little model, actress. After being on complete bed rest from 5 months on, my lil Sugarbear, Jaclyn made her arrival. She was a beautiful, tiny sweet thing. I was not supposed to have any more children, nor did he want any. I however prayed to God, if I'm ever pregnant again, I'd love a blonde haired, blue eyed little boy! God is so good; I was pregnant with Parker. I was faced with the reality of doing it without Jack. I would not terminate. Things got a little scary as I had to have a lump removed from my right breast when I was 4 months pregnant. I did it under a local as I didn't want to risk losing this miracle baby boy. I had my tubes tied so I was not at FAULT for getting pregnant again. Colleyville became our new location to live as he wanted kids in public school, not private. His feeling were you can write off taxes not tuition. In hindsight, our kids would have done much better in smaller classrooms. Life goes on at a fast rate of speed, especially with four amazing, good looking, smart, athletically gifted children. It's club soccer, competitive cheer, dance and more soccer. What an absolute blessing each of my children truly have been. After 20 years of marriage to a narcissist it finally came to an end.

In January of 2016 a lump popped up in my right breast. I was tired and under a lot of stress. I assumed it was because of an increase in caffeine, so I cut back to 2 cups of coffee in the morning. The lump did not go away. In March, my kids and I were awakened by the home alarm at 3 am. As my kids walked out of their rooms with their cell phones, I was flipping on lights and trying to figure out how to turn off the system. It was so loud; panic began to set in as I ran from room to room trying to figure out the cause. As I reached the guest bedroom and bath, I saw the flames shooting up outside the windows. As I ran out screaming "fire!", the glass was shattering behind me from the extreme heat. I yelled at my kids to get out, we grabbed the dogs, got in our separate cars, pulled into the street. I realized our cats were still in my bedroom. The police officer Patrick, a friend, would not let me go back in. I said they're in my master bedroom, the other side of the house. Unfortunately, they perished. It was devastating to us as we loved our fur babies like family. All we could do was sit and watch our beautiful home burn with six different departments there. It was a total loss so we had to go to a hotel. The following day, Tuesday, I was scheduled for knee surgery. I decided to go through with it in spite of everything going on because as a dental hygienist, I had already rescheduled my patients which I love and wanted to keep the consistency I could give them. The Wednesday after my surgery, early evening, I was lying in bed with my leg elevated when I get a call from my oldest daughter crying. She had just been in an accident rushing back to Dallas from helping me and hydroplaned on 114. I had one daughter go pick up Brittany and her sweet lab, Kelly, waiting on the side of the rainy highway. My other daughter had to pick up Parker at Cowboy Stadium. I have never felt so helpless in all my life.

We moved into a townhome and were settling in when I received a call from nurse Natalie. My oldest daughter had called her about the lump. You need to get in for a mammogram. For the first time in my life, I had no health insurance. She told me about CAREITY.ORG. {my story is on their site} I called them; they were amazing!!! I was set up for my mammogram that week and the next week the biopsy. Two days later I got the call, you have Invasive ductal carcinoma. Wow, sucker punched in the gut. You begin to cry and your life flashes before your eyes. My first thought, my kids. Careity had me set up at The Center for Cancer and Blood disorders in Ft Worth. I truly believe God had His hand in this all along. Isaiah 40:29 "He gives strength to the weary and increases the power of the weak." I learned it was Triple negative breast cancer and I said I'm not going down without a fight!!! I had all tests done, my port placed and I began chemotherapy. I completed two treatments and was unable to do the third week because my numbers had dropped. I was devastated. I had a shot and left the center. I had 2 additional days of shots to boost my system. I was baptized at Compass Christian church that weekend. 2 Corinthians 5:17 "If anyone is in Christ, he is a new creation. The old has passed away; behold, the new has come". I returned the next week determined to continue my treatment. I did my blood work and the numbers looked good so onto the exam with Dr Robyn Young. She did a visual exam, palpated, measured, looked at the computer, re-examined I mean looked hard, NO LUMP!!!!! With a tear in her eye she said, "It's gone!" I said GOD IS SO GOOD!!!! At that very moment I had PEACE!!! I know He is in control. He can change our MESS into a MESSage, Our TEST into our TESTimony. I believe I'm a walking miracle, I know I'm on a mission for Him. I completed chemo, did a double mastectomy due to BRCA1 gene and reconstruction with the best plastic surgeon, Dr Vishnu Rumalla.

I truly thank God for allowing me to share OUR STORY. I want to continue to shine His light and be an inspiration for others. Don't ever give up, He is always with you. May you too find PEACE, as I have while living in Texas with four great kids, a son in law and a precious grandson. May God bless you all and live each day to the fullest!

Email me @ Brenda_zimmermann@yahoo.com

CHAPTER 3

TEARS THAT HEAL

KATHY GREMILLION

2,007 nights with little to no sleep, consumed with nightmares, stressful dreams, night sweats, a tear-stained pillow, sheets with smeared makeup used as a tissue when all were used up, silent pleas, and sometimes outward pleas to God. For over five years, 2,007 nights took a toll on me and every aspect of my life. Was I just at "that age" I would hear people talk about when you don't sleep well anymore? Why did it seem like I was suffering so much more from sleep deprivation than most people. One of my doctors referred to it as "war torture", and for me, it was torture. I considered myself as having strong faith. I prayed and went to church much of my life. But none of this seemed to help. I felt guilty for not praying harder or getting up early to read my Bible.

Suffering through the day, not just physically, but mentally, became my normal and lasted for years. Suffering from depression most of my life, sometimes the sadness I felt was like a darkness that hovered over me, but this time, it was different. I had only felt this a few times before in my life. The darkness didn't just hover over me; it seemed to cover me from the outside in to my core.

This time, I didn't speak to anyone about this darkness. In fact, I tried to hide it behind smiles. I was serving at church, even though at times it was so consuming, I thought it would win. As I sat in this former church that Sunday morning, a place that I should have felt peace and comfort, all I felt was the darkness and pain. The mental pain was so bad I had a plan: suicide. I had it planned out: I would write a note to the church telling them I had my own name, not this one's sister or wife, and this woman with the name Kathy that was hurting so deeply. It seemed like no one noticed me or my pain, for that matter. I would stand on the altar and say, "I bet you see me now," and then, end my life, right there on the altar, in front of everyone. I didn't have a day when to go through with this plan; I just had the details worked out. The next Wednesday night, I was back at church. My depression was so strong I could no longer hide it behind a smile; my demeanor showed it this night. After service, I waited outside, leaning against a pole as if I couldn't even hold myself up against the weight of this dark place. One man made a comment in passing that I looked stressed. My friend, Melodi, from church asked me to go have coffee with her on Saturday, and I accepted her invitation, not knowing it would be such a life-changing moment in my life. We met that Saturday morning, and as I sat across from her, she started to tell me things that I knew without a doubt were a message from God! "I sense a spirit of suicide" were her words. I sat astonished at what I just heard. Remember, I had not spoken a word to anyone about my thoughts or even my depression. God, in His perfect timing, met me right there at that coffee shop that morning and showed me that he saw me when it felt like no one did, He loved me, He was for me, and He had bigger plans for me. Satan thought he had a master plan to destroy me, but I belong to THE MASTER of the Universe, the king of kings, the one who not only knows my name, but knows every hair on my head and has my name written on the palm of his hand. "See, I have engraved you on the palms of my hands;" Isaiah 49:16.

Looking back at the suffering of being scatterbrained, having headaches, being nauseated, lack of motivation, and fatigue were so severe it would impair me at times. It would be traced back to even further than I ever thought. I had been on depression and anxiety medicine much of my life and later diagnosed with ADD and took medication, which all helped. There was a piece of the puzzle no one seemed to be able to figure out. I spent years going to doctors and running tests like blood sugar and thyroid, which all came back normal. Years of talking to different people, trying to figure out if anyone else felt this way. In my desperate attempt to find an answer, I found that deep inside me, the complex parts of my brain and my body were holding on to some stories, that either I chose to file away or that my mind filed away because the pain, shame, or guilt was too much to bear. TRAUMA made a name for itself in my body, my brain, and my life. Trauma, for me, was a slow-eating disease. After years of trying to find that missing piece of my mental health issues, I was diagnosed as having PTSD. I was somewhat confused, because I had been through several hard things in my life and survived. Like many, I had associated the term PTSD with veterans. This diagnosis sparked my interest, so I did some of my own research and uncovered so much about how trauma related to so much in my life. I had faced many difficult battles of different kinds. I am not exactly sure when the trauma started, as I am still in the process of working through it. Depression and anxiety have hindered me much of my life.

At the age of nine and ten, I was put in a mental home for adolescent because my doctor had no other options on how to deal with my separation anxiety and fear of school. The hospitalization, in itself, was terrifying for a nine-year-old little girl. Followed by several other traumatic life events. I thought I survived. Now I know I was just stuffing them down deep and not really surviving them at all. My brain was storing each event that would eventually need to be processed to heal. According to Dr. Daniel Amens, "Your brain is an organ linked to the rest or your body." Just the magnitude of the exhaustion I felt was enough to think something had to be physically wrong with me, and this was not just in my head. My brain and body were storing years of trauma, affecting me mentally and physically, and I was stuck. My condition was more than the depression, anxiety, or even my ADD diagnoses. It was more than a choice to be sad, angry, unorganized, forgetful, and more than the stigma that mental health conditions are self-inflicted and, therefore, carried shame and guilt.

I learned that grief is not just in loss, but also the loss of something significant. The summer of 1990 was an exciting time. It was the summer before my senior year, and I was in my oldest sister's wedding, and she was the first in my family to get married. We never would have never imagined that the same beautiful bride we watched walk down the aisle in June, would be laying in a hospital bed that September unsure of her future and with a lot of unanswered questions. It was supposed to be a simple surgery, and since I was in school, I didn't go to see her the day of surgery. When I saw her the next day, I barely recognized her because of the swelling. A month later, she passed away. I can still remember that somber day so vividly: the yellow gown she was in, still warm to my touch, the light coming through the window with the curtains that were opened for the first time since she had been there. Most of what happened after is a blur, but I know that I did not get to grieve her death. After she was gone, I rarely remember her name spoken. Not talking about her seemed like the way to cope. I was dealing with it the best I knew how at the time. Grief will show up in different, unhealthy ways if it is stuffed down.

In August of 2016, I faced a different kind of loss. A weather system dumped trillions of gallons of rain in our area and caused what was called "the great flood". Me, my three children, and my two-year-old grandsons lost our home, most of our belongings, and pieces of our life built over years. It was not just a physical loss; it was a loss of the safety and security of our home. I went through a range of feelings from sadness to anger. Seeing what felt like our life in a pile of ruined things that took years to get but was destroyed in a matter of hours was a huge loss on so many levels. In the midst of the flood, as I sat sweaty and worn down from cleaning out not just stuff, but parts of a life that lay ruined, soaked in dirty, muddy water, I broke and cried out in agony, "Why God, why!" Days after the grievous task of cleaning out our home, I sat alone on the porch swing of our sweet little house with streams of tears running down my sweaty, dirt-stained face, staring at the huge pile of the ruined parts of our lives as it stared back at me. I just didn't understand, so I got up from the swing, and as I walked up to what felt like our life in a pile of ruin, I asked again, "God, why?" And right there, in that moment of such extreme loss, God spoke to me and said, "I wanted you to throw your old life away." Wow, what a profound answer with such deep meaning. What I considered loving words from the Father who wanted to restore and renew me and my life through this tragedy. People will say "be strong" in the midst of loss. I think strength is allowing yourself to feel, not being ashamed or feeling bad for having an emotion. Emotions are healthy and healing when processed in a healthy way. To cry, get angry, to talk about loved ones who have left us even if it brings up sadness and even fear when it is managed in a healthy way. It is recognizing your emotions, even speaking it out loud, identifying where it is coming from, what it is saying, processing it, then giving myself permission to feel the emotion. Sometimes, we need to have a good cry and not feel like its weakness. We need to grieve a loss by talking to safe people about the sadness it has caused. John 11:33-35 says, "Jesus saw her weeping, and he saw how the people with her were weeping also; His heart was touched, and He was deeply moved. 'Where have you buried him?' He asked them. 'Come and see, Lord,' they answered. Jesus wept." Jesus wept; this is the shortest verse in the Bible, but what powerful words! In a time of grief, Jesus shed tears. God, the almighty powerful, creator of the Universe, in the flesh wept in grief. Tears are not a sign of weakness. Tears are healing and a sign that something we loved and cherished is lost. Tears can be a move of compassion. They are unspoken hurt too deep for words. Thank you, Lord, for the beautiful gift of tears, that you not only see the pain and sadness behind them, but you collect them in a bottle, each teardrop gathered up by your mighty, loving hands. Psalms 56:8 says, "You keep track of all my sorrows. You have collected all my tears in your bottle."

I could have easily been overlooked that day at this church that thousands attend. But that day in April, as I left service, tears streaming down my face, I was met in the lobby by Rachel, the pastor's wife with such compassion. Asking for help has not always been easy for me, but that day, the words just spilled out. Going through an especially difficult time. I needed counseling, but at the time had limited means to get the help I so desperately needed. She took my information and soon afterward, I received an email from her, checking on me and was put in the loving hands of Mrs. Shelia for counseling. She walked with me through this difficult time with guidance, love, and prayer. I'm convinced that meeting Rachel in the lobby, filled with people, that day was not by chance. Like the woman who was so desperate for healing and Jesus found her in the crowd, Jesus saw me that day in the crowd desperate for help. Matthew 9:22 says, "Jesus turned and saw her. 'Take heart, daughter,' he said, 'your faith has healed you.' And the woman was healed at that moment."

In his remarkable way, God led me to this church with the name Healing Place Church, a healing place for a hurting world, that is now my home church! God will find us in those desperate times when tears show our pain or even when the only prayer we can speak is "Help me." Psalms 40:1-3 Why are people so hesitant to get help for mental health issues and care for the most important, complex organ in our bodies, the brain? I have many times heard people say, "I don't need or I don't believe in counseling" or "I don't need or I don't believe in those types if medicine, but try to cope in unhealthy ways." Depression, anxiety, sleep deprivation, and trauma have hindered every area of my life. I went through times I thought I didn't need help. I tried to convince myself I was okay and could control it if I just thought more positive, exercised, prayed harder, read certain books, helped others more, just tried harder. I tried all these things, but still struggled then I felt guilty I couldn't "fix" myself. All these things are helpful and some are a very important part of health and healing, but no one thing alone healed me. I needed help from a professional that specializes in mental health, a program geared towards trauma. I needed emotional help from a therapist and spiritual help from God. There is courage in seeking help, in surrendering to our needs and admitting we need help. There is no life when the brain is not functioning and no life when our hearts are apart from God. A revealing of sadness, anxiety, and trauma through therapy is like working out the pain in physical therapy due to an injury.

In Matthew chapter 4, many people sought Jesus for healing from various diseases and suffering. Jesus was a healer for them, the great physician, another word for doctor, the term coming from the Latin word for teacher (Isaiah 9:1-7). I am in awe when I look back, no matter if it was circumstances from life events, the bad choices I made, or the circumstances that left me broken at the hands of another, God never left me. He sees me, and He has big plans for me! Ephesians 2:10 says, "For we are God's masterpiece. He has created us anew in Christ Jesus, so we can do the good things he planned for us long ago." In the words of Dr. Martin Luther King, Jr., "Only in the darkness can you see the stars." What a beautiful picture of how through our darkest times in his perfect timing, God's light will shine so bright we will know He is there and always has been.

A few years ago, I visited a church for their Ladies' Night Service. I thought I was going to listen to a message, but that night, God, in his amazing ways, gave me a beautiful, direct, prophetic message through Pastor Beverly Bilbo, that has helped me to believe that God is very present in my life. "Kathy, God did not create you to fail" was part of the message spoken. Many circumstances of my life and the lies of the enemy made me believe different. Trying to undo the damage of hurt from the hands of others and life, my own bad choices, and believing I failed has been a relentless battle to get my life back. I received care for my mental health, being seen by a doctor for medicine management. I started going to an outpatient treatment facility for PTSD treatment, I continued counseling, continued to have my good support system from safe family and friends, learned to manage my emotions in a healthy way, self-care, exercise, and eating better; (I need to work on this; I do live in south Louisiana, where the food is amazing), I was finally sleeping again after five years, and GOD! Please don't hesitant to get help. Even Jesus needed help carrying the cross. You deserve help if your cross is too much to bear. I must admit I was hesitant about the vulnerability in telling my story. But as I wrote, I asked God "As I picked up the pen to write, take my hand and guide it to be His story told through me". The Word says healing comes by the words of our testimony. In my prayer life, I often say, "Thank God this is not the end of my story!" Maybe it was just the beginning.

I am Katherine Gremillion, the proud mom of three amazing children, Maranda, Carlie, and Garon, and a loving MiMi to two grandchildren, Maddixx and Noah. I am engaged to my best friend, James. I am a Cajun girl from South Louisiana, a trauma survivor, and I have a heart for the hurting and mental health awareness, and I love the Lord.

Contact me at Kathy.gremillion@icloud.com

CHAPTER 4

VICTORY

JUDY PINEGAR

One dreary day, I found myself looking up from my position on the floor. My ex-husband had grabbed me, dragged me about six feet, and had thrown me across the kitchen floor, up against the appliances, making a loud noise. My youngest son, Larry, was in his bedroom. I could sense when I was in danger or if one of the kids was in danger. I knew Larry was safe this time, but I was not. I was laying on the floor, up against the stove, with my ex-husband standing over me with fury in his eyes. I told him to go check on Larry. I said, "I think this must be scary to him." He went to check on Larry, and I ran out the back door and down the street to my parents' house. I was ridiculously protective of my ex-husband and had never told my parents just how bad things were. I thought I hid the abuse well, yet my parent knew something wasn't right, even though I tried to hide my pain.

I met my ex-husband when I was 11. He lived across the street and became the son my dad always wanted. We married one week after my high school graduation. I was 18 and so excited!

Nineteen months later, in 1966, our first son, David, was born. I now had my own Betsy Wetsy doll. He was a 24/7 job. It's not like when you are a little girl, you can play with your doll and put it away for days. I was so enamored with him, and it did not take me long to adjust to being his mother. Three-and-a-half years later, Larry was born. He was small, cute, and very blond. With David, I had to work outside the home as soon as I was able. I didn't work when Larry was born, and David, Larry, and I were so happy to be together each day.

The boys' dad would not get up with them in the night, and encouraged me to let them cry. He rarely changed a diaper. He would not babysit for me to do things I might enjoy. Life was all about him. He had boats, fishing gear, golf clubs, four different trucks in one year, and ANYTHING he wanted. David and Larry wore rags (when rags were not fashionable) to school, and I wore hand-me-downs from my sister.

Being in a marriage where my abusive ex-husband had multiple affairs through the years, I found myself and our sons physically, mentally, and emotionally abused. I think he was jealous of our son's attention from me. Once, he used a belt on one of our little boys' legs, and it left an imprint of his name from the belt. These were days in the wilderness. Very dark days, indeed.

I was married and mostly abused for 27 years. You might ask, why did you stay? I am a Christian, and I don't believe in divorce. Secondly, how do you send a little boy's dad away? Thirdly, I believe in prayer, and every day, I thought God would make him a good man, husband, and father. God was working on him, but my ex had other ideas. Unfortunately, there's free will. We have choices that we make here on Earth, and some of our choices hurt others and come with consequences.

We had brief good times that would cause me confusion. One time, I even got to hire a maid after an episode of his infidelity. That was nice! During the times of his involvement with other women, there was more abuse, and he refused to go to church. The cycles would continue each time with more abuse. My self-esteem was destroyed. He said, "No one would have you if I left," and he said, "You are fat." I weighed 100 pounds. He would throw me around and across the room. He would shake me and talk abusively to me, all while sleeping with other women.

A particular incident I remember with horror was him hitting Larry, at 17, in the chest and verbally abusing him. My ex kept looking at me and saying, "What are you going to do about it?" He would hurt the boys to hurt me. I was so scared of him, and I knew if I moved or said anything, it would be worse for Larry. David would try to stand up to him sometimes, which made his situation terrible. One time, my ex was kicking Larry in the backyard, and David got between them and said, "Leave him alone. If you have to kick someone, just kick me." Larry learned to be more passive with him, which helped him some. Nonetheless, Larry was abused.

I have struggled with guilt and remorse. Instead of protecting my boys and myself, I should have called 9-1-1 several times. I didn't know how to leave. It makes me want to cry just writing this. What good is guilt and remorse? We can't go back and do a thing about our past. Let's not limit our future by dwelling on past mistakes. We are *not* defined by our past. Forgetting the past and living for today is a prerequisite for a healthy future. In Philippians 3:13, Paul says, "Forgetting what is behind and straining toward what is ahead," is what we all have to do. Remember 1 John 1:9, which says, "Confess our sins, and He is faithful and just to forgive us of all of them." Only when we turn loose of guilt and shame can we live in deliverance and VICTORY.

Be a blessing to others along the way and provide hope in the midst of their storm. I learned many lessons through this nightmare, and I want to help others who are suffering. There is victory and deliverance after abuse and struggles of any kind. God teaches us lessons in everything we experience. Romans 8:28 indicates that, "All things work together for the good of those that love the Lord." I claim that scripture for David, Larry, and for myself.

A funny story is that I learned to be creative when I stood bold in the Lord. One day, I hooked up a recorder to our home phone, long before cell phones. I would leave the house, and he would call the "other woman". Like children, they talked about me, her husband, their sexual experiences, and planned their rendezvous. I listened to the tapes and lost eight pounds in the first eight days of listening. I don't know why I listened; I think it was disbelief or a part of my journey to reality. During one conversation, they were planning to meet in Bethesda, Maryland. My husband was going to the post office training center. I heard her exact itinerary, so I waited until it was the day before the trip and said, "Honey, I have a surprise for you. I am coming to Maryland next weekend. We have always talked about seeing the Smithsonian, and we can do that over the weekend." He said, "Oh no, you can't do that. You like Las Vegas. Why don't you go to Las Vegas, instead?" I said, "Oh no, I have already purchased my airline tickets. I am coming on Friday at 2:00 on American Airlines Flight XX and fly home on Flight XX the next Monday." Since I had overheard them talking about their plans, I quoted her same schedule as my own. I made it look like she and I were traveling on the same flights. I thought this was hysterical.

Now let me tell you, he was not happy, and he began sweating. As soon as I left the house, he was on the phone telling her to cancel her flights, and she did. I hoped she did not get a refund.

Then, my parents and I flew to Las Vegas for the weekend and he sat in Maryland all alone, thinking I was going to show up. I did take the time to call from Vegas and said, "Well, I took your advice. I am in Las Vegas having a ball."

In the last few years of being married to him, I remember saying, "Satan has taken over his whole being." He did not even look like himself. My mom has the ability to discern good and evil most of the time. She came to the house one day, and the next day, she said, "The presence of evil in the house and in him could be cut with a knife." I had a Godly African American woman friend who had taught me that the name of Jesus and the blood of Jesus are powerful. She said, "You can bind Satan up in the name and blood of Jesus."

I was reading my Bible regularly, which made him mad. He said something mean to me about God. I said, "That is a lie of Satan." Well, that infuriated him. He jumped out of his chair and put his hands around my throat and said, "I am going to kill you." So, with his hands around my throat and looking into my eyes right in my face, I said quickly, "Satan, in the name of Jesus and by the blood of Jesus, I command you to loosen your hold on me and get back over there and sit down." I felt like I was looking into the eyes of the devil. He melted, took his hands away, and went and sat back down. This happened two times.

Through the years, I begged God to change my husband's heart, to make him a good man, husband, and dad. I even advised God on exactly what to do and how to do it. Now you know God does not need me on his advisory board. If faith could have changed things, He would have changed. Every day, I woke up and thought, *Today will be a good day*. That was ridiculous on many levels. God does answer prayers. Sometimes, he says yes, sometimes, no, and sometimes, wait because he has a better plan.

After my husband spent our 25th wedding anniversary in Atlantic City with "the other woman", enough was enough. I had a talk with God. It was the fall of 1990. I got down on my knees and I said, "Father, I will stay in this marriage the remainder of my life if that is what you want me to do, but I am frightened for my life. I feel in danger daily, and my sons have been abused. Father, I am weary and tired. I would really like it if I had a husband who is a strong Christian man, who loved and cherished me, faithful and loyal, and would love my sons and grandkids." Then I said, "HOWEVER, THY WILL BE DONE, NOT MINE." I prayed this, and I meant it. I SURRENDERED my Will to His Will. Consider PRAYER and SURRENDER to God's will in all you are going through. Let God direct your life.

On February 4, 1991, my husband left me for the "other woman". Even with everything, his leaving was traumatic for me. It should have been the happiest day of my life. However, I married for life. I believe in marriage. I believe in working out any difficulties. I believed it would be forever. I know that sounds strange. I should have been elated, but I cried and cried after he left for the last time. I was fearful and didn't know what my future held.

Here comes God's plan and answer to my prayers. I was upset, so I went to eat with a girlfriend, she took me to the Waterfall Restaurant in Addison. I did not want to go home, so we stayed after eating. The place had a dance floor, and I was asked to dance by lots of men. I always wanted to dance, so I did. When one of the men was dancing with me, I cried as we danced and told him, "My husband left me today for another woman." His name was Jim, and he was so kind. He persisted over the next few weeks in asking me to dinner and even sent me flowers for Valentine's Day. I hadn't been treated nice in years. I was still married, so I asked different people what I should do. My co-workers had witnessed the abuse and said, "Go." I asked my mom and dad, and they said, "Go." I asked my Christian counselor, and he said, "Well, the husband is the head of the wife." He said, "Ask your husband if it's okay with him." Strange thing to advise, but I called my husband up and said, "This man is asking me to go to dinner, is that okay with you?" His response was, "I don't care what the hell you do, just leave me alone." Wow, now I had permission to go to dinner with this man.

I told Jim I could go to dinner. I had not been on a date in 27 years and had never dated anyone but my husband. I was scared. He picked me up at my parents' house. They got a copy of his driver's license and even sneaked out to copy his license plate. We even evaluated his divorce paperwork to be sure he was single, LOL. He took me to a nice restaurant by Bachman Lake with a dance floor. I was reluctant about going on any date with anyone, so I had my co-worker sitting at a nearby table watching over his every move. He was charming, polite, and quickly gained my trust. Jim and I have been married for 27 years as of 2020.

Jim is *all* I prayed that I wanted in a husband. He is a Christian; he loves and cherishes me. He is loyal and faithful. He loves and cares about my sons and my grandchildren. He is always ready to help. Every day with Jim is better than the day before. I thank God every day for this blessing. He is my Promise Land experience.

Through these trials and tribulations, my faith has grown. We grow more in the valley than on the mountaintop. It becomes easier the next time we hit a bump in the road of life to trust God and know he is working. Romans 8:28 says, "All things work together for the good of those who love the Lord". Scripture indicates that nothing is impossible for God. Proverbs 3:6 says, "In all your ways acknowledge Him, and He will make your paths straight." One thing to remember: if Jesus is your co-pilot, SWITCH SEATS.

I know that God uses all the struggles we encounter to mold each of us and shape us into who we are today and enable us to be a blessing to others. Just because the past did not end up like we wanted it to, doesn't mean our future can't be more than we ever imagined. Ephesians 3:20 says, "He is able to do immeasurably more than we ever ask or imagine." Let us not look back, but seek Jesus first and let him direct our futures. Satan wants to weigh us down with guilt and make us miserable. God has a plan for each of us today and tomorrow. Let's get on with HIS PLAN on our path to VICTORY.

I am Judy Pinegar. I am married to my best friend, Jim. I have 2 amazing sons, 3 stepsons, and we have 14 grandchildren. I love the Lord. I am a prayer warrior and I am happy to help other women understand the presence and unconditional love of Jesus. You can contact me at jpinegar1@verizon.net.

CHAPTER 5

RESILIENCE OUT OF REJECTION

MARION THOMPSON

Where do I start? From the beginning, or from the middle of mess when Jesus Christ came to rescue me? He whispered, "I love you." It was sweet, and I have never heard a sound like this since that very day. It is a wonder in life when we look at others, and think they have it easy. That's God, not allowing others to see the journey that it took for you to get where you are today… in the present. Oh! Let's not mention how He will blind others of your future because the enemy is always busy to steal, kill, and destroy. This is when you discover that you are an OVERCOMER.

FAMILY

Sometimes we start out in life in some hard situations with family. Family can try you or break you in ways that you cannot believe you carried this burden. Misunderstanding, lies, and lack of faith in where God is taking you, or what He will bring forth in your life isn't something that can be seen or believed when you are in the fight. The fight to change your life when you grow up. Your very own parents, friends, and others that are close to you will grieve you with their doubt. It doesn't matter if you work hard, or if you are dependable—people will continue to think what they want concerning you. This is why you need to maintain a relationship with God—no matter what. The Word says, "When my father and mother forsake me, then the Lord will take me up. Teach me thy way, O Lord, and lead me in a plain path, because of mine enemies. Deliver me not over unto the will of mine enemies: for false witnesses are risen up against me, and such as breathe out cruelty. I had fainted, unless I had believed to see the goodness of the Lord in the land of the living. Wait on the Lord: be of good courage, and He shall strengthen thine heart: wait, I say, on the Lord." (Psalms 27:10-14) We all have heard they mistreated Jesus. What makes you think that we will not experience the same?

You can be in a place of struggle, and family will be faithful to remind you of your place. *The one that always needs help is not going any further than where you are.* You can't give in to the feelings of lack and a low self-esteem. You have to rise above the thoughts of wanting to hide or separate yourself from them. Sometimes, the people who love you do not realize they're a pawn in the enemy's game. Everyone plays their part, whether it is good or bad—just know everyone has a role in your life. It hurts when opposition *is* the person who is close to you as family, but you can't lose family due to this. This is key: people are going to do what they do. There are disappointments they bring to you, but don't forget there is joy in allowing others to have their roles in your life. Not everyone will disappoint you. When family forgets that words hurt, just remember that God listens. He is forever watching, and He feels your hurt. God sends others throughout your life that love you as family can or should. Don't lose hope in this.

There was a time when I had to start over more than once, learn how to walk all over again, and learn to trust others. Despite all of this, God kept sending a Word or a person that showed me He had not forgotten about me. *God has not forgotten about you!* He allowed people to step into their roles of helping or doubting enough to toughen me up even more. The hurt was there, but I can tell you love and peace outweighed the hurt. We have to study the Word, because this is what holds you together when life is rough. God has all the answers.

FRIENDS

Let's take a moment to reflect on friends… they are the ones we expect the most out of in relationships. We believe our friends should know us and they are family. But they can stab you in the back and blindside you. Have you ever had forever friends? Faithful friends? Or the ones that you least expected to hurt you deeply? All of the above is what I have experienced and through Christ, I had to overcome the impression left upon my life because of friends. Friends that have cut deep only make it harder for those who truly love you. In spite of all, you have to remember Christ is the only true friend that we could ever have. God is forever, no matter how much we want friends to stay in our life or treat us better. This is not going to happen, because everyone has their role to play. God loves you so much that He reveals a person's character to you. What you choose to do with it is what determines your outcome in that particular situation. Isn't it amazing when He loves you so much to take the blinders off your eyes to see a person for who they are? The Holy Spirit has rescued me many times in my thoughts or my fears of what I was accepting from others… what I was choosing to allow them to do. You have to love yourself the way Christ loves you. Despite it all, God also teaches us to forgive others. We have to separate the spirit from the person…acknowledge how the enemy is just using someone to hurt you. They are helping to build the foundational work that God is doing in you. How can you know what you can handle until you are tested? How many times will I have to go through? Am I failing? Did I pass? God only knows. I can tell you He is revealing the person God is building you to become. You are strong, and you can take on anything, as long as God is with you. The Word says, "What shall we then say to these things? If God be for us, who can be against us?" (Romans 8:31 KJV). *Everyone* can be against you, *but* with *God*, it doesn't matter. He renews you over and over again, and when situations come up, our responses are different. When we choose to walk in Christ, our thoughts aren't our thoughts anymore. God makes us handle things differently than what our flesh wants to do, *if* we *listen*. There are some moments when things are hard, but remember you have come too far to turn back. Your enemies want to be proven in what they have said about you behind your back or to your face. Make them a lie… you should choose to *live* and not die.

FAILED RELATIONSHIPS

If I had a dollar for every time it didn't work out… not a hundred, but a dollar. There were so many along the way that have made you realize your mistakes, and others you can't burn out of your memory, no matter how hard you try. Don't kick yourself any more than someone else wanted to hurt you. You can't continue to beat yourself up when God has forgiven you. I know this for myself, and He has given me rest, despite my feeling that I should have known better. God wants what is best for you and for me. This is what we are waiting on- the *best*. Not what a person wants to ration out to you. Are you a pet? A beggar? No! You are a child of the MOST HIGH! The child of the ONLY TRUE LIVING GOD. God does not ration out His love to us, and why should you believe this is what you deserve. God's love is without any reservations. I can tell you from experience of living in hell and sin, it took only God's grace to come and free me. Thank you, Jesus! But yet,

I didn't forgive myself. I had spent a decade hiding behind the curtains of being a workaholic to not cope with renewing trust. The enemy can make you feel that no one could love you, but it is a lie. Every person that was not right was because we wanted to believe they were, despite what we were being shown by the Lord. Remember when I said that God loves you so much and that He listens? He heard our prayers, and He created our future before we were born. Why should we expect to be with person who will not be an investment into our future? God always yields a harvest. Do you think a mighty work is for the weak-hearted? You belong to God, and He knows who can handle the work that He has planned for you and me. What I am saying to you, I had to tell myself this very same thing more than once. Guess what… at first, it was not easy. Then, it became necessary to humble myself to what God wants for me. When you follow Christ, what He wants becomes what you want for yourself. Don't just tell others that you trust God, walk the faith walk, proving that you trust Him. No matter what.

LOOK to YOUR FUTURE

Times are hard, it doesn't mean that you are failing. It just means that God is proving to you that He is bringing you out. No matter what it looks like, you can't lose hope. This is what I have made sure to impart to my sons as they were growing up. We experienced struggle, but they experienced me giving up hope. I say to my sons, "The enemy wants to make you quit. God is omnipotent, and He will answer you. We have to talk with God. You have to have a relationship with Him. Mama can only take you so far, but God will take you all the way. No matter what, don't quit. If God allows you to wake up the next day, it is another opportunity to change. Don't give up on yourself, and don't pay attention to anyone else who doesn't believe in you. That goes for your Mama, too. Don't ever become so deep in your despair that you feel all hope is lost. It is never lost. The devil wants you to believe this, and this is how he takes lives by making them feel as if there is no hope." My sons would reply, "Yes, Mama, I know." I would say to them, "Whenever God takes me home, do not be angry with Him. It was my time, and we all are on borrowed time. You should just know that God allowed me to go to Heaven to be with Him." They would reply, "Yes, Mama, I know." As they got older, I would say, "Mama loves you, but God loves you more!" The same reply would come from them, "Yes, Mama, I know!" Why did I say such things to them? Because they had to hear it from their mother. They had to hear that despite what happens in life, even if they ever experience losing the one they love, God is always with them. Too many people experience the deepest hurt and harm themselves, because they do not know how to release it. Many have yet to understand that life is hard, but the Word is life's answers to navigate through it daily.

Every time someone or something held you back, God made you overcome it. Every time your struggle became greater, God was elevating you to another place in Him. Every time the ones you love left you desperate for answers and hurting, God was taking you deeper in His love. Every time you had your back against the wall, bills higher than you could see your way out of the money pit, God showed Himself to be Jehovah Jireh. Every time your thoughts took you through a depression state, He became your Jehovah Rapha. Every time when others tried to make you feel that you'd never amount to anything, God was your Jehovah Nissi. Shout to the Heavens what God has said about your life! You are an OVERCOMER. You are a WARRIOR. You are a CONQUEROR. You were born to WIN, not fail. There is no failure in God. What legacy can I leave with you? What Word can I give you during this time when all our faith is being tested?

>God is able.
>
>He is the author and finisher of your life.
>
>He is your deliverer.
>
>He is your keeper.
>
>He is the restorer of your soul.

He will make your enemies your footstool.

He can give you what you ask for when it lines up with His will.

Stop thinking that He doesn't want you to prosper. He wants you to prosper!

He created you in His likeness, so this means you are not ugly or dumb.

Stop acting as if God makes mistakes, because He doesn't.

People make mistakes. He just loves us enough to give us room to *choose Him* by our own free will.

I will leave you with this thought... you were meant to read this book at this very moment in your life. If you only knew how the fire was turned up when each of us agreed to write a chapter. If you only knew how the author, Alyssa, had to keep having faith for this book to reach the world. If you only knew how she had to believe that each person would come through, or have faith for funding. Every person had to contribute while the fire was burning. Every person had to believe God while in a fight of their own. God gave us all grace and tender mercy... just to write the pages, to reach your heart, to touch your soul, to give you answers to what you have been believing God for. You can't faint or quit. You were born to win, and you are who God says you are. Speak the Word only – what God has to say about you.

I love you in Jesus Christ. I stand for Jesus yesterday, today, and will stand for Him tomorrow. There is no room for watered down Word. No room for doubt. God is the answer to all of our problems.

Follow Me: Marion-ZKS Enterprises on Instagram

CHAPTER 6

FINDING THE ROOT

EMILY EHE

Do our thoughts really matter? Do we really have the power to change them?

I've probably always known that to some extent that yes, thoughts matter. Growing up, I often heard, "Take captive your thoughts" coming from 2 Corinthians 10:5. So if *God* is telling us to do that, I figured it must be possible, but how?!

And to complicate matters more, how can one possibly know which thoughts are *okay* and which aren't? In childhood, I often heard to think on whatever is lovely, pure, right, and true (Philippians 4:8). But how are we to know if our thinking does that? Of course, if I'm thinking of *murdering* someone, that's obvious. Not a cool thought. That's a thought I need to work on changing. If I'm cursing in my head, I knew that didn't fit into any of those categories. But what about the thought that says, *I'm a failure.* The thought appears true, so it must be true. Or what about the thought, *There's something wrong with me.* If it looks true, it must be valid, right?

Imagine with me a young girl of six who has just finished Kindergarten. She overhears her mom saying, "She knew her ABC's going into Kindergarten and came out not knowing them. I talked to the neighbor lady who's a teacher, and against homeschooling, and she said, 'She's never going to make it in the public school.'" From then on, the little girl was homeschooled. But what did that little girl *hear*? *There's something wrong with ME. I can't even handle public school, like everyone else.*

The little girl had caring parents and two younger brothers. So, she always joked that she was the family guinea pig—the test run— being the oldest. She was close in age to her siblings, and they got along fairly well, though she always wished she had a sister. Playing cowboys and Indians and building forts were okay, but playing with dolls was better. Her brothers weren't big fans of playing house. Plus, they always ripped the heads off her Barbies and poked the dolls' eyes out. She saw the comradery her brothers had as kids and wished for the same. She longed to have a sister to share a room with and talk to.

As she got older and into the teenage years, she wished for a sister even more, as things were getting bumpy with her parents. She didn't know what to do with this change that was happening and desperately wanted someone to talk with about it. She noticed her brothers seemed to avoid these bumps and run-ins. Was she defective? Was she broken? Was she a failure as a daughter, too?

Every week, this same girl would help her mom by cleaning the house with her brothers. This was part of her chores. Each week, she'd try her hardest to clean it well. Almost every week, she'd learn about how she missed *this spot*. So, next time, she would make sure *that spot* was taken care of, only to learn of a different spot. I'm sure her mom just wanted her to show her daughter how to do an excellent job at whatever she applied herself to, but the young girl received a different message, *I'm not good enough. I can never get it right.* It's also important to note that the Christian environment she was in, at the time, was not one to give compliments, as it might make one proud. As a result, the feedback she was received throughout her childhood was, unfortunately, one-sided.

When it came to schoolwork, she did alright, but sports? That was another story. To be fair, the only sport she ever participated in was T-ball. The reason for this was, she thought she wasn't good at sports, like the rest of her family. When it came to family baseball games, she'd always miss catching and hitting the ball. Whenever a ball was flying towards her, she'd close her eyes and hope for the best, so that might have had something to do with it. Her parents encouraged her to keep playing baseball with the family. She did, but never saw the progress. So, she just began evading sports to avoid embarrassment. The same thing happened when it came to drawing. She tried her hand at it, but could never make it match the drawing book, even a little. She desired to be good at drawing and art, but thought it was something you were gifted with or not. And in her case, it must be not. So, once again she quit, when art was no longer required at school. She was bad at sports and drawing. That's what she believed, so she stopped trying, all because of her thinking.

Jump forward a few years, and the now adolescent girl doesn't remember hearing she was beautiful. When she looked around and compared herself to others her age, she thought she was heavy. Her mom would comment if she gained or lost weight, which she interpreted as she really must be heavy. When she observed her clothes versus those of her peers, she saw a big difference. Their clothes were cute and stylish. Hers were not. Additionally, she noted as she got a little older–other girls got noticed by boys, but not her. She must not be beautiful, if the boys didn't notice her, right? On top of that, she didn't hear "you're beautiful" from other people, and she doesn't see it herself. (She would, in fact, be in her early 20s before the first time she remembers someone calling her beautiful). These experiences and her observations established what would become deep-rooted thinking in her for years to come: *I'm not beautiful.* Sadly, she took this as truth until her late 20s.

Sometimes, the emotional pain would become so much for this little girl, she'd cry alone in her room and ask God to take her life. It seemed to her to be the only way out. She didn't see any answers or options anywhere. She felt so alone, stuck, and hopeless. She'd pray and pray, asking God to help her, but it seemed to fall on deaf ears. Nothing was changing for years. So, if she was still so hopeless *with* Him, then God taking her life must be the only solution. Everything she tried didn't work. She must be defective. I mean that had to be it, right? Because God was perfect, the problem couldn't be Him, and therefore, it must be *her*. The prospect of living an entire life feeling this broken and defective seemed too much to bear. She knew she couldn't take her own life, so that's why she asked God to do it. It seemed the only way out.

Do you identify with this girl? I do, on every level, because that little girl is me. I was constantly bombarded with thoughts of, *I'm not good enough, there's something wrong with me, I'm broken, I can't do anything right, I'm a failure, and I'm defective.* I didn't know any better at the time. My observations told me they were true, so I took them as truth. I learned many years later, that children don't have the skillset yet to process such thoughts on their own and discern whether they are true or not. As a result, they just take their thoughts as truth and don't question them.

Sadly, thoughts like these and so many others pass through our minds daily, and we never stop to question them. Why is that? If you're like me, it's because you don't know they aren't true or that there's even a way to stop such thinking. But where do thoughts like these originate from? A good number of the thoughts going through your head may be following you from childhood, too. Mine did, because I never questioned or challenged them to find the actual truth. The thoughts that plague you today as an adult may have come from incidents on the playground as a kid, a bully at school, or simply an offhand comment from someone—a teacher, parent, or sibling. Unhealthy thinking can be sparked by something we heard either directly or indirectly, things taken personally that were not personal at all, or messages that you internalized and heard differently than the sender meant for them to be received.

What about you? How do your thoughts affect you? It might be easy to brush them off and think, *Come on, they're only thoughts.* For many years, I did just that. But now looking back, WOW! Instead of questioning these thoughts and rooting out untruths, I was believing lies. The lies of *There's something wrong with me and I'm defective* kept me from participating in sports, which my husband tells me I'm not half bad at. The lies that *I'm not good enough and I'll never get it right*, kept me from pursuing my dream of drawing, which in the last few years, I have begun to dabble in. And people tell me I'm actually decent at it! This same line of thinking also kept me from pursuing photography, which I enjoy tremendously.

You want to know what kind of thinking this is? Stinkin' thinkin'! My stinkin' thinkin' didn't only keep me from drawing, sports, and photography, but also from believing I was beautiful. The stinkin' thinkin' was rooted so deeply it took years of hearing "you're beautiful" from people consistently, before I could actually even start believing it. You might be thinking, *Okay, but those thoughts had fairly minor impacts on you overall, no? So, you didn't become an artist or photographer. And so, you didn't like what you saw in the mirror. What woman does? Is it that big of a deal?* My thinking unfortunately didn't just keep me from pursuing my talents and interests, being at ease in my own skin, and questioning my value—it also kept me from developing resilience, grit, and perseverance. Consequently, if things were hard and I wasn't good right away, I'd quit or not even try to avoid failure or embarrassment. Many people as an adult form friendships and have fun together via sports, but I refused, for fear of being embarrassed. This line of thinking kept me feeling left out until just recently. The belief that there was something wrong with me, made me guard and hide certain parts of me, even in simple ways, such as expressing myself and laughing out loud. And WOW, my stinkin' thinkin' of *I'm a failure, broken, and I will always be this way* kicked me in the gut HARD when I got married. But that's a story for another book.

In short, all of this toxic thinking kept me from being fully me and who God intended me to be, until I started finding the root behind the behavior and not just placing a Band-Aid or quick fix on it. Every struggle we have—overeating, acting out sexually, overreactions, the list goes on— has a root somewhere. It's important that we take time do the hard work, dig deep, and find the root. It's also of immense importance in this process to ask our Heavenly Daddy to reveal it to us. And please, never just focus on behavior modification. There's no freedom and life to be found there.

By now, you might be saying, "Okay, okay, so now I know my thoughts really matter. But you still haven't told me how can I know if the thought is true, lovely, right, or pure? How do I know if it's a thought to keep or throw out and replace with truth?" Read along with me to find out. First and foremost, one always needs to compare their thought to the Bible and see if it matches up. Sometimes, that's easy to discern, for instance, take my example at the beginning of the chapter. If I'm thinking murderous thoughts, the sixth commandment clearly states that we should not murder. Pretty straightforward. Now, let's look at something not so straightforward, the thought, *I'm worthless*. You may look around you and circumstances appear to tell you it's true. It may even appear that some people seem to think it. So, is it a true and right thought? Or is it a thought from the enemy, trying to take you down? Let me answer that for you— it is a thought from the enemy to take you down!!! How do I know that? One reason I know that is that God's voice tells us that we are fearfully and wonderfully made (Psalm 139:14). Something that is fearfully and wonderfully made isn't worthless. Furthermore, we were bought out of slavery to sin for a high price (1 Corinthians 6:20), a price that cost God His Son. Something bought at this high price definitely isn't worthless, but instead, it is beloved and of incredible value! One of my favorite tests for the voice in my head is inspired by Romans 8:1, which says there is therefore now no condemnation for those who are in Christ Jesus. Condemnation is a big word that just means strong disapproval or criticism. Therefore, if God doesn't think I'm worthless or have strong disapproval towards me for who I am or what I've done, then I can know that voice is a lie and one I need to replace with truth. Knowing how to do that practically eluded me for many years. Just trying to erase a thought isn't enough. About six years ago, I learned we can't just erase thoughts, but we have to override that thought with a new thought. It can be as simple as repeating the truth to myself, out loud if possible, over and over and over again. As many times a day as needed. For me, that looked like when the thought *I'm worthless* came creeping around, I'd start saying to myself the truth: *I'm fearfully and wonderfully made. God doesn't condemn me, so neither should I.* It's not a quick fix, but it's transformational and worth the work. A few years back, I learned the power of positive self-talk and that takes captivating thoughts to a whole new level, but for now, I need leave you with this.

While I have not gone through physical or sexual trauma, which are awful, and unimaginable, I have experienced emotional trauma in my life. Emotional trauma is still trauma. There are no physical wounds. No tests to be done to prove it. No one sees any physical marks. Therefore, it often gets overlooked, dismissed, and minimized. It isn't talked about. Leaving the individual experiencing it to question and second guess everything happening to them. I want you to know that if you are have gone through emotional trauma, there is hope and a path forward.

There is a Heavenly Daddy who loves you so much and wants to bring you healing, if you'll let Him. How do I know this? Because I've seen it over the last few years for myself in my own life firsthand.

I want you to know there is a good chance that without Jesus and a personal relationship with Him, I wouldn't be here today. He is the one I turned to in my journal over and over again. I may have had more questions than answers many times, but deep down, I always knew He was the real deal. There were just things I didn't understand yet and slowly over time, He's provided the answers. It hasn't been easy, but it's been worth it. If you find yourself thinking you're stuck and things are hopeless, please know there is hope. You are not alone, no matter what you are going through. THERE IS HOPE! Don't forget that!

Emily Ehe was a classroom teacher in a low-income area for five years, after leaving the business world. She also had the opportunity to teach English in South Korea. She is fluent in Spanish, loves to go country dancing when she has time, and enjoys the outdoors. She is a photographer and painter. She enjoys walking alongside women who find themselves in a tough place and need encouragement and support. Which is what led her to lead at Re: generation as well as share her story of God's grace in her life from the stage. She has also been given the opportunity to share her story at Equipped Disciple. She is passionate about turning around stinkin' thinkin' and finding the root of issues and not just placing a Band-Aid or quick fix on it. She lives in Dallas, Texas with her husband, Pierre. She would be grateful if you gave her a like in the Facebook world (Emily Ehe) or followed her on Instagram (finding.the.root).

CHAPTER 7

ROBE OF STRENGTH

KIMI WEBER

"Please don't leave me, please don't leave *us*, you can't just leave your family." I imagine that is what I yelled out as he drove off. I just stood there, sobbing on the driveway, until my neighbor took pity and came over, wiped my tears, hugged me, prayed over me. I am sure I was quite the sight sitting there in the fetal position on the concrete, in my pink terry cloth bathrobe that was covered in spit up, breast milk, and my goodness, had I even showered that day? I suppose if you are going to pick a day for your husband to leave you, you would try to pick a day you could have at least showered, put on some makeup, looked a little cuter, perhaps gotten out of your bathrobe. There I was, a complete mess, looking as pathetic as I possibly could as he just drove off. *How on earth did we get here?*

Looking back on that morning, so many years ago, I remember waking up so happy. I had been working on the whole gratitude thing through a Bible study, and I'm pretty sure that exact day I thanked God for "birds chirping". Yep, the day he left, I had been in some sort of fairytale I suppose, bulleting in my gratitude journal, birds chirping, precious baby girl, precocious toddler boy, a beautiful home and family. Everything seemed so perfect, but it wasn't at all. I sat across from him, this grumpy stranger who had become so distant, and asked what was wrong. I remember saying, "We have everything going for us, so what on earth is wrong with you?" And then the words came out of his mouth, that I'll hear forever, the words I carried for years in my heart and possibly into every relationship, "I'm just not in love with you anymore." So, I did what broken people do, *I'll hurt you before you hurt me*; I told him to leave. Did I actually tell him to leave? Did *I* put this in motion? That seems to be what he told everyone. Maybe I was daring him to go? It's as if he had been waiting for me to say that forever, like he needed permission. He stood up, went into the closet, packed his bag, went into the kids' rooms to say goodbye, and left. He just left.

I'm not sure when my rejection issues began, but I have always seemed to have trouble with people leaving. I had all the love one could ever need from a family. I always knew I was adopted, and my parents made me feel so special, as if I was chosen off a shelf at the toy store, their most prized possession. So that November day, in my early twenties when I had found my birth mother and set up a meeting. I was full of anticipation; I remember getting ready for the meeting like I was getting ready for prom. I'm pretty sure I imagined her as a movie star all my life. A movie star would be too busy to raise a child, and she was probably out there being famous all this time. But you see, I met her, we exchanged hugs and looked at pictures of our lives and what I learned was that she was, well, just, as normal as the rest of us. She had me at 24. Surely, a 24-year-old could certainly take care of a baby. You see, my other theory growing up was that she was a teenage mom, and had to give me up for adoption because she was just too young. Oh, wait, she *didn't* actually want to take care of me. She proceeded to tell me she chose the alternative to adoption, but a friend came and stopped her just in time. So, at that moment, the room was spinning and Satan grabbed a foothold; and then, although at the head level, I could say, "Wow, girl, you are really meant to be here, God's got big plans for you, Sister," instead, seeds of rejection took root. Maybe I wasn't wanted after all. Maybe I'm not worthy. Maybe people leave you because you aren't good enough. I am certain at some subconscious level I had seeds of doubt of who I was. I certainly had trouble accepting who I was in Christ. I guess if I had it all figured out then, my life would have been pretty boring over the past couple decades. Instead, I have been on a journey of finding truth, God's truth for my life, and it has been a beautiful story He has woven together for me.

You see, I hypothetically stayed in that pink terry cloth bathrobe for longer than I needed. That girl left on the driveway needed to shed that thing so fast and put on the full armor of God and march into being a single mom. But she didn't. She got so caught up in drama and pain that it consumed her. She was caught up in being "left". Our mind can play dangerous tricks on us, if we aren't grounded in faith. One thing happens, and before you know it, there are seeds of unworthiness and rejection planted in your wounded heart. So, here's what I want to shout to everyone standing in brokenness at this moment. Let God heal you. Let Him penetrate your heart and pull you out of the pit. I did this time and time again, pit after pit, but it took a long time. My path to freedom took every detour it could because I was so stubborn and my faith needed work. I did the dance with God, and He never left me. I would take two steps forward and ten steps back, for years. I clung to scriptures through all of it and tried desperately to believe God's promises. We are never going to have the perfect life—there will always be troubles, and our God will all always be faithful. Know this in your heart and soul. Feel it in your bones. He is the God who stays!

I had the foundation and several tools to walk confidently in Christ, but I just couldn't seem to execute when my world blew up so many years ago. My heart so desperately wanted to trust the Lord completely, but shame and unforgiveness stood in my way. I have never felt more like a failure than after my husband left. All I ever wanted was to be a mom and a wife, but there I was, feeling like I was damaged goods. Every time my children left with my husband, then to become ex-husband, I felt abandonment and anguish, as if salt was being poured in the wound over and over. I wondered how on earth could I do this on my own? If I wasn't enough for the man who vowed to love me forever, then how could I be enough for my children?

One evening, when it was "his" first weekend to take the kids, before we were divorced, I watched their little faces as I closed the truck door. This was the first weekend I would not be with my baby, the first time I couldn't feel her breastfeed and feel her heartbeat next to mine. My son put his little hand up on the window. I fake smiled and waved until the truck was out of sight. After they were gone, I walked into the house, into his room, and collapsed onto his bed sobbing. His cowboy room, this work of heart and art that his dad and I created together, was the best big boy room. The house was so perfect, the walls, the halls, everything had a place, but it was empty, and I have never felt more alone. I finally pulled it together enough to go to bed, but first, I took my Bible and opened up on Proverbs 3:5-6 on my chest, asking God to be with me as I slept and show me what to do. That was the first of many nights I would cry myself to sleep with my children gone. But in the middle of the night, as sure as a phone ringing or doorbell awaking me, I heard in my broken heart as clear as day, *"Kimi, I'm going to take care of you and the kids."* I sat up, eager to hear more. *God, is that you? What do I do? How do I move on? Is my marriage really over?* Nothing more. And how thankful I was for just that audible in my heart. The peace that came over me was all I needed. I knew somehow, I could go on. And I would.

I didn't give up on my husband coming back. I prayed daily, with a whole slew of dedicated women at the Baptist church praying, too, but one day, I asked my mentor, "How do I pray about this?" She said, "Honey, you have to pray for God's will." This was not easy. This was going to take some growth on my part. Yet, there God was, holding my heart and hand every day. I'll never forget being on my knees next to my bed, asking God if my marriage was over, and Him whispering to my heart, "Yes."

It made perfect sense that I should get baptized. I had never been baptized as an adult, and it seemed like a good plan to start new. Turmoil was all around me, but my babies, my heartbeats, they needed a strong mom and deserved one, too. It is by no accident that on the day I was getting baptized, in fact, just a couple hours before, I received the news and confirmation of what my gut had been telling me. *There was another woman.*

Okay, so let's do this. Dunk me down in that water and when I come back up, make it all disappear, right? Cleanse me, Lord. Take *all* of it. No. That's not exactly how baptism works. I was professing my love of Christ and making it known who my personal savior was. Yes, there was cleansing, but more importantly, it was a rededication of my faith, I am not alone. I will never be alone. And so there, in the midst of turbulence, my faith in God would keep me steady.

I would like to say that after my baptism, my walk with Jesus was effortless and easy. How different life would be if we just jumped right in step with our dance partner and let Him lead, staying in the grip of His will, but for some reason, I wanted to do it all *my* way, on my own strength. Reflection is something I have spent years doing, yet I have yet to figure out what about surrendering is so difficult. Why did I hold on to all the hurts and pain for so long? The same hurts, unforgiveness, and shame that I left at the foot of the cross years ago. How many trips back there did I need to go? The answer is daily. We have to go back and hand it over to him every single day until one day, it's *all* been handed over, once and for all. Take note, friends, God has all the time in the world. He remains on the throne for all of eternity. Sometimes, I imagine him just shaking his head every time I crawl back to Him saying, "Oh my child, I knew you'd be back. Let's try this again."

As I found my way and learned how to do Plan B, I was not alone. I still stand amazed at how my Heavenly Father, the architect of my life, carefully designed and orchestrated so many things. He gave me exactly what we needed at all times, always providing and always loving us through it. There was joy, there were smiles, and there was happiness. I was blessed abundantly with my parents to help me coparent with friends, neighbors, and teachers along the way. But it was hard. Divorce is not fun. I marvel at those who make it so amicable and look so easy. I prayed for peace. It came in tiny spurts. I never imagined what was coming. Days were long, and I missed having a partner. I so desperately wanted to give my children a stepfather and complete our family. That right there, that mentality, I know that the enemy was at work again, telling me I was not enough on my own.

I thought I found exactly that. The life partner I had waited for, the love of my life, the one who would stay. He was a good man, but sadly, as much as he seemed to love my children and me, he had an addiction bigger than that love for me. That loss broke me, but you see, when you have a stronghold like rejection hanging over you, Satan uses every bit of it to worm his way and get you completely off track. Through the years, I have learned that what seems like man's rejection is only God's redirection or protection. We often don't see all of this until much later, after we come out of the rubble and out of the refiner's fire. But sure enough, time and time again, I can look back and see that my Lord and Savior knew exactly what He was doing. He would be the one who would walk with me through the valleys. The one who would never leave me.

Just when we think we have learned our lessons and have adequately grown our faith; the toughest storms seem to hit. There was a big one, when my kids were teens, that affected my whole family, taking us all into the fire for the fight of a lifetime. A child custody battle that would crush spirits, break hearts, but eventually bring God glory! It's not my story to share, just yet, but God truly had the victory.

I am here to tell you, friends, that God is good all the time and all the time, God is good. Only He can create beauty from ashes. That broken woman on the driveway wearing the pink, fuzzy, stained bathrobe years ago got up. She got up every single day to raise her children. She got up when she wanted to stay in her sadness. She got up and held her head up high when she felt insecure or overwhelmed. She got up and shed that robe of rejection and traded it in for a robe of strength, a "garment of praise, instead of a spirit of despair", and now, she is "clothed in strength and dignity, and she laughs without fear of the future." God continues to love her and bless her abundantly, in spite of her imperfections. She knows she is His, a daughter of a King, the God Almighty. He loves her, and He loves you, too.

My name is Kimi and I am a proud mom of two amazing, beautiful children named Luke and Landry. I have been an elementary school teacher for 23 years and find so much joy in teaching little ones to read and write. My prayer for those reading this is that you know you are loved and adored by a living God. May you feel His joy and peace wherever you are in life and trust Him with your future. The best is yet to come!! Feel free to contact me at kimweber70@att.net. Smile and Hugs!!

CHAPTER 8

DIAMOND SEASON

AMAKA OJIRIKA-NZERIBE

It's diamond season! Diamonds are formed under pressure, and they are rare. The cut of a diamond is a difficult process to endure, however, we must go through the fire. Think about this: do amazing results come from laid back encounters? I think not! As diamonds, we will definitely go through high temperatures (trials) and will withstand pressure, because I, too, have gone through tribulations that have enabled me to come out as pure gold.

I am from Nigeria, Africa. I came from a polygamous family, and I had nothing. Growing up in Africa as a female and also left-handed was difficult—it is taboo for a female to be left-handed. I went through hell, because I was the only left-handed person in our family. At the age of seven years old, I remember my mother took me to the hospital, and they put a cast that is bigger than my little body on my left arm, so I would be forced to write with my right hand, but I would not give in. I would go to school and cry all day long, and the teachers would tell me, "Get ready to cry blood out of your eyes, because you must write with your right hand—that is the culture." One day, we went to church, and the priest asked my mom if I broke my arm. She responded, "No. We did that because she is left-handed, and it is an abomination for a female to be that way." The priest finally convinced her that was a gift from God that she should not be angry with God. She finally let me be. I moved to the United States when I was 23, and lived with my father. My first job was Braums, earning $5.25 per hour. I was super excited to have my first job. As well as, when I came to the U.S., I discovered how I wasn't the only person who was writing with their left hand. I felt like this is where I belong. All my life, I wore a garment of shame. Being accused of so many things and often feeling hated by so many in my family, because I was the black sheep, I didn't realize I had a gift, and that was why the devil was attacking me. I was unhappy, carried a burden on my shoulder, cried a lot, felt lonely, and even hated the world. I had nowhere to turn to, nor even had a soul to express myself to.

On November 27, 2006, I came back from work feeling bitter, and I began to cry. I got on my knees and began to tell the Lord, "I have heard of you; however, I do not have the relationship with you as I would like to have with you. After I cried, "O God", I began to ask the Lord, "Are my sins so much greater than the others who have sinned that I can't be forgiven?" In the midst of me crying, I began to tell the Lord to search my heart, and I told him I am broken, and believe it or not, there was a light that had shined into my bedroom. When I realized there was a light shining, I then felt a peace that surpassed all understanding. Meanwhile, I was in a relationship with a surgeon, but I wasn't happy, because was still void. I later learned that I was born with a hole in my heart, and it had been opened since birth. I had no symptoms, and I exercised twice a day and worked countless of hours. Nobody but God who could have been carrying me and yet no symptoms. On January 7, 2007, I had heart surgery, and it was very successful. God revealed to me that He placed that particular surgeon in my life, so that I could receive the best care, and He showed me that He was here for an assignment over my life and canceled the relationship.

In May 2008, Jenkins (my husband) called me out of nowhere. I knew him from Nigeria because he was a friend of the family. We gained a closer relationship for six months by talking over the phone. All the way from Nigeria, he proposed to me over the phone. I thought he was insane, because we weren't in a physical relationship. Something told me to say yes, but I thought to myself, *How can I marry someone I have never dated?* On April 18, 2009, I went back home to Nigeria to marry my husband, as our marriage is still a mystery. God heard my plea and moved on my behalf. He took care of my heart surgery, canceled a relationship that wasn't in His plan, and handpicked the man He ordained and blessed me to be in a union with. Not only did He take away the garment of shame that I carried over the course of my life, but He replaced it with a garment of peace, joy, and favor. God took me from feeling like a nobody and moved me to being a princess and marrying me into a royal family—my husband is a prince. We have three beautiful children.

My husband came to the United States in February 2010. Let me be transparent with you, just as I began to be so happy, my life became so chaotic. My trials and tribulations enabled me to have a greater experience with God as I went through the fire. I even had physical pain in my back and was basically paralyzed while carrying my third child. My doctor told me if I didn't get to the hospital before I delivered my son, I would die, because they wanted to be available in case I had complications. As we were driving to my doctor's appointment, my pains became closer and closer, and my husband and I had to pull over at 7-Eleven ten minutes away from making it to the hospital. When we pulled into the entrance of the 7-Eleven, my husband had to call the ambulance. The dispatcher couldn't understand the street name over the phone, because out of his fear, his accent became thicker and thicker. He even had to go into the road to be able to see the sign and spell out the street name. While he was taking care of that, there was an older lady who appeared at my passenger car door in a wheelchair, wearing a white gown. The people at the 7-Eleven couldn't see me, but I could see them. While the lady sat silently looking at me, she never said a word. She was there until everything was done. As soon as I went into the ambulance, I looked at her, and she looked at me, and she was gone. I asked my husband and two kids, "Did you see that lady?" They said, "No" at once, and I knew then that God sent an angel to be with me. My water didn't break, and I didn't even push out my baby, but he came out still inside the sac. The ambulance drove me to the hospital, and when we arrived, my doctor asked me was I the one at 7-Eleven where the ambulance came. I responded, "Yes." He was at the restaurant close by, waiting for the hospital to call to see if I had arrived, but instead, I delivered him in my car at 7-Eleven. I named him my miracle child.

After I gave birth to my son, I then realized that I was born with a gift—that is why I was tried by the fire in the early years of my life. Just like I birthed my child through pain, I see how a diamond doesn't shine at the beginning, but over time, with pressure, it becomes refined. I realized at this point the Lord enlightened me that I was a light and He needed me to shine for His glory. I began to think about how Shadrach, Meshach, and Abednego went through the fire, but when they came out, they didn't smell like smoke. On September 14, 2019, I came back from work, and my husband turned on the news, even though I don't watch the news. It was on Fox 4 News, and a family was asking for prayer for an 11-year-old girl. She went swimming on a Labor Day weekend and contracted a brain-eating disease called amoeba, which was contracted from the lake. I then added her to my prayer list, because I was already interceding on other people's behalf. God literally instructed me to leave my living room and go outside, so that He could give me instructions on what to pray concerning this little girl. I went outside, and this was the first time ever hearing the voice of God. He began to give me instructions on what time to leave the house and what I should wear for the day (all white). I asked God to show me a sign. Before I left, I immediately saw a purple and blue rainbow on the wall. I never heard the voice of God so clear. I quickly drove to Cook's Children Hospital in Fort Worth, Texas. I asked God, "How are they going to know who I am?" He said, "When they see you, they will know exactly who you are." When I arrived, I walked to the chapel, and He told me to pray whether I met the family or not to pray over the young girl. I went upstairs to try to find the family, however, since I wasn't an immediate family member, the nurse wouldn't allow me to go back to see the family. I then went back downstairs, and God asked me to go on Facebook, and I saw a girl who happened to be her cousin talking about which floor the little girl was on. I went back up to the second floor, and the family told me to go press the button, but when I pressed the button, the nurse still wouldn't let me come to the back, where her family was. I didn't know that was her family sitting in the lobby and the Lord didn't want us to meet at that present time, so that He could prove to me that I am God. At that point, I gave up, and my coworker, who was new, texted me out the blue and asked me what was I doing. As I stood under the tree, I replied and proceeded to type about my crazy mission impossible experience with God that I had that day. Four people came out from the hospital, and the lady told me, "You look like an angel." I said, "Thank you," and I went back to texting with my friend. The family walked a little bit, and the guy who was her father asked me, "Who are you here to see?" I walked closer, and I began to tell them about my mission from God. And behold, they told me, "We are her parents." We both stood there and cried from this experience. I knew that there was a true and living God. In June, I requested to leave early from work by 11 a.m., not knowing that was going to be the day for her funeral. God plans things before He manifests things to us.

I definitely realize how strong God made me to be and how resistant I was from the pressure of the trials and tribulations I had to endure. I want my readers to understand that whatever you are going through, do not give up: there is still hope. Miracles happen every day, and God can use anybody. No matter how bad your situation may be, if God can bring me out of what I have gone through, then I will say He will do that same thing for you. I have fought a thousand battles, and I am still standing. I have even cried a thousand tears, and look, I am still standing. I have been broken, betrayed, abandoned and rejected, and I am still walking as proud as I can be, laugh loud, live without any fear, and even love without any doubt. I am beautiful, and I have learned to be humble.

Proverbs 3:15

She is more precious than rubies, and all the things you desire cannot compare with her.

CHAPTER 9

OVERCOMING DARKNESS

ROBIN THURMAN-BRENDLE

When I was first asked to contribute to this amazing book, full of magnificent women, I was terrified. My mind immediately went to the dark and insecure places, as it tends to do. Thoughts started running through my mind, "*I'm not good enough.*" What could I possibly add?" "*People are going to judge me*". You know the part of the brain where everything you write or say is wrong or sounds just a little too crazy? That was me. I thought to myself, "*Should I even be doing this?*" To think, I almost didn't participate.

The usual panic and anxiety set in. I was honored and humbled to be asked, but wondered, *Why me? Why my story?* So, I prayed. I asked God to help me understand these "whys", and it came to me. I'm not alone in my experiences. I'm not alone with my anxiety. I'm not alone with my depression. I'm not alone with my PTSD. Maybe, just maybe, I might be able to help someone. It's not easy to write about my personal life and to put myself out there. It's not easy to say, "Look at me, see how crazy I am." But I'm not crazy!

People with severe anxiety and depression have to deal with it every day and try to put a smile on their faces in front of other people. To be honest, it's quite exhausting and terrifying. It's something I deal with every day; I know I'm not alone. Even as I sit writing this, I'm having an anxiety attack. I want the chapter to be perfect, meaningful, and helpful.

I know it's never going to be perfect; life isn't perfect. I live my life with the motto "perfectly imperfect". I want others to feel that they aren't alone. I want to keep them from falling into the same traps I have; go to the dark places I have been in my life, and still go to more times than I care to admit. I want to help others who are suffering and show them how to make it through to the other side; maybe with a little scarring or some bumps and bruises, but make it! That's not an easy task for me to do, because most of the time, I don't even know how to get through it. But with the grace of God, I'm here, still trying to make it and working to improve myself every day and deal with the demons that try their darndest to get to me. There are times that they do make it in, and it's the hardest thing in the world to cast them out. Then I think of the people who love me, who care for me, who want me to beat my demons and go to God for help.

It hasn't always been this bad. The fact is, I've had a pretty good life for the most part. Everybody has their struggles, problems, and issues, and it's scary, but as I look back, my life has been pretty good. Not always, but whose life is perfect? I've always had a roof over my head. I have a fabulous family, a wonderful husband, and three amazing fur babies (now two—I lost one a few weeks ago while writing this. I'm still not over it, but here I am, opening up, knowing that I will once again see my boy, Nomad, at the Rainbow Bridge). My dogs are my children, because I'm unable to have my own biological children, which is another story in and of itself.

I admit I had a difficult childhood. I grew up with divorced parents, who tried their best, but were never really there for me. I don't think I have ever said that out loud, or have written it down, but I felt like I was raising myself. My sister and brother, 12 and 10 years older respectively, were a lot like my parents, as they were relied upon to babysit me a lot, but when they moved out, I started rebelling.

I guess that's when I started going astray and walking, sometimes running down a dark path. My family didn't go to church. I was never taught much about God. In fact, I'm just really starting to learn about God and the Lord Jesus Christ. I was captured by something other than the light and the goodness. I couldn't begin to tell you what that was, but it wasn't good. I didn't know it at the time, all I knew was that I was having fun, doing things that a teenager probably shouldn't be doing, and having no repercussions from it.

As I got older, I started to realize that there actually were repercussions for my decisions and my actions, and they were not pleasant. This is also about the time I went off to college in another state. Looking back now, I think I was looking for a clean slate where very few people knew me, and I guess, in a sense, trying to run away from everything in my past. Who knew that I would end up doing the same things and becoming the same person I was before I left Texas?

So, that's a little bit of my back story. A crazy, rebellious teenager who thought that she could run away from her problems and start over. I found that to be a HARD NO. You can never run away from your problems, but you can learn how to deal with them. However, I didn't do that in the beginning either. I still tried to push them under the rug and continued down the path of darkness.

College is pretty much of a blur to me. I was your "typical" college kid, doing what college kids do. Partying, drinking, hopefully making it to classes, and praying that I actually passed those classes. It was at that time that I was diagnosed with major depressive disorder, severe anxiety, PTSD, and at one point, with bipolar disorder. That's a lot to deal with when you're barely 21 years old and don't even understand what half of those mean or how they affect you. So, you take the medications and go about your life. No counseling, no discussions, no nothing, just, "Here's your medication, and take it as prescribed." A great deal happened during my college years that I won't go into—just suffice it to say, I was not thinking about God.

After I left college and moved back to Texas, things didn't change much. I knew I wasn't feeling good about myself. My depression had gotten worse, my anxiety even more severe, and I felt like a failure. I had spent so much time and money trying to get a degree and failed. I tried to start different careers and failed. I had been in several relationships and failed. I was, in my own eyes, a complete failure. That's when the most toxic things in my life took over. I reverted back to what I knew and that was the dark path. There was no light in my life. I had gained weight, lost all self-esteem, and was still taking a cocktail of medications for mental health illnesses that I knew nothing about. I was at a breaking point.

I quit taking my medications and then spiraled out of control. I didn't know what was happening, but I knew I needed help. From where that help would come from, I didn't know, but I was lost. I was in a dark cloud and couldn't seem to find my way out. This was me for the majority of my life, until about ten years ago.

This was and has been the worst and best decade of my life. In 2010, I was in probably the most toxic relationship I had ever been in. By this time, I had zero self-esteem, so much self-loathing I could barely look at myself in the mirror, and such severe depression that I thought

I didn't deserve anything good. And I didn't have anything good. I was knocked down even more by the man I was dating. I was being emotionally, mentally, and physically abused, and taken for everything I had; both monetarily and emotionally. I was called the most horrible things and treated like I was nothing, and I felt like nothing. Cheated on, stolen from, you name it, it happened in this so-called relationship. I was completely believing that I deserved nothing, was nothing, and contemplated suicide on more than one occasion.

Then, one day, I got a message, on Facebook nonetheless, from a guy I once dated in high school. We had spoken and seen each other off and on for several years before I was "locked" in this toxic relationship. I would tell him about the things that were going on, and he knew I was in a bad place. He knew something was wrong in my life, because I was not the same person, I had been five years earlier. He saw and heard the difference in me. He was literally my savior, because he was the one who opened the locked door of that toxic relationship and let me out. He did what I could not do on my own and helped me to remove the abuser from my life. I'm elated to say that my "savior" is now my husband, and we just celebrated our six-year wedding anniversary. It was then that I started to think that there was something else in play here. There was something else out there that put my husband in my life at that particular time. It was then that I started to truly believe in God.

Although I had a narcissistic abuser out of my life, I was still emotionally and physically in pain. Even with the abuser gone, I was still abusing myself. I didn't have any positive coping mechanisms to deal with the damage that had been done and the coping mechanisms I *did* have were extremely destructive. The only way I knew how to cope was to not cope. I drank a lot of alcohol, so as not to think about the pain, and I began cutting myself, so I would only have the physical pain and the emotional pain would then dissipate. I was not healthy physically or mentally. No one in my life knew of this destructive behavior, because I was very good at hiding it. This toxic relationship that I thought was over was not even close to being over. He may have been gone, but the damage was done.

During the end of this toxic relationship, I was also dealing with a major surgery and was in the hospital for two months, due to complications. My mother never left my side for the entire two months of hospitalization, and my brother was at my home, making sure my abuser didn't take away my fur babies. I started to feel lighter, despite all of the trauma, and I had an "awakening" of sorts.

As I was coming out of anesthesia from my second surgery—or maybe it was during the surgery I can't be sure—I saw my father, who had passed away a few years earlier. He told me I was going to be fine, that it was not my time to go, and that he was always watching over me, and I actually felt his presence. It was the most amazing feeling in the world. It was not just my father, though. There was another presence around me. One that I had felt, but never knew what it was. It was God. I know it was God. This moment changed my life forever.

I was not a religious person. I believed in God, but in the dark part of my brain and the self-loathing inside me, I didn't think God believed in me. I didn't think I deserved God's love until that very moment. How wrong I had been my entire life! He had always been with me. In my heart, walking beside me, sometimes carrying me, but he was always there. That moment was the turning point of my life, and I have never looked back.

Throughout the last eight years since then, I have been in and out of the hospital more times than I can count. I had numerous surgeries, tests, was poked, prodded, you name it, and before every procedure, I would pray, because I knew God was with me. Yes, there were times that I wanted to give up because I was just so tired of being in pain, but that's where the grace of God, my faith, and support system became the most important things in my life. They never gave up on me, even when I wanted to give up on myself.

My best friend from college—I call her my earthly guardian angel—sent me a bracelet inscribed with the words, "Fate whispers to the warrior "You cannot withstand the storm", and the warrior whispers back "I am the storm." That precious gift was exactly what I needed, and I can never thank her enough for everything she has done for me. Just as I can't thank my husband or my family enough for always being there and supporting me, no matter what.

Having a plethora of mental, physical and emotional issues is a scary thing and something I will have to deal with for the rest of my life, and I've come to terms with that. But I think back to the inscription on that bracelet and remind myself, *I am a warrior, and I will beat this storm!* Not by myself, but with my faith in God and my family.

I would like to thank everyone who encouraged me to write this chapter. I was terrified to put myself out there; to relive some of the worst times in my life and when I thought I wouldn't have a life. This has made me dig deep, talk about things I didn't want to talk about and gave me hope! I'll be honest, I cried *a lot* while writing this, but I would not change it for the world. It was worth it, and if anyone can relate to my story, or if I give at least one person hope, or help in any way, it is all entirely worth it!

I pray that all of you will feel the light and follow your own path through this crazy thing called life, no matter how long it takes and the hardships you may endure. I promise you it's all worth it, and everything you've been through makes you stronger than you ever thought you could be, and let me just say it's the most amazing feeling in this world when you see, feel, and experience the beautiful light and love of the Lord!

My name is Robin Thurman-Brendle. I am an Independent Styling Consultant. I love helping people feel more beautiful than they already are. Contact me at robin.brendle@outlook.com. I am here to help those struggling with their mental health.

CHAPTER 10

TO GOD BE THE GLORY

SHARRON RIVERA

My earliest memory was when I was about 3 years old. I remember getting upset with one of my brothers about something and my dad overheard and asked me if I wanted to get out of the car. What I was thinking in my 3-year-old mind was I get to stand up for myself and I get to choose to be bold and independent. I had no idea that my dad putting me out of the car on the side of the highway and then driving away would be as traumatic as it was. I remember my dad driving off and I was so scared…traumatized. I said to myself after that traumatic event, "I will never speak up for myself again." I was all alone. My family abandoned me.

My parents made sure to have us in church and my dad would read the Bible to us when we would stay home from church or we would listen to Jimmy Swaggert on TV. We would do most things as a family. We all played sports. My two older brothers and younger sister were always the popular kids in school. I tended to gravitate toward the less popular kids in school. The ones that would accept me easier. I remember wearing hand-me-downs and getting boxes of used clothes from other families. The clothes most of the time would not fit but we were so thankful for the kindness and generosity. I also remember a trip to get school clothes and seeing how worried my dad got when we were at the counter for him to pay. I spoke up and said we can take my clothes back because I did not want my dad to worry. I also remember not having much food and my mom secretly applying for a Texaco charge card to buy food for us so that dad would not find out. Those kinds of things would make them fight.

My dad and mom loved the Lord. We lived in a small town in Antlers, Oklahoma and my dad would take us into the woods to help him cut down trees for firewood. The most amazing things would happen when we were all gathering the wood and playing and joking with each other too. It was the feeling of being accepted and that I was part of the family. I still would struggle though because my thinking was always a little off. I would have thoughts that I was just a little different than my two brothers and sister. I struggled with why I could not be clever with my come backs like my brothers and sister would have with each other. My mom and my dad did not seem to be as proud of me either.

My parents really enjoyed sports. My oldest brother would make up games for us to play inside and outside of the house. We would play school inside and my oldest brother, Larry, would ask us, "What's a hypothesis?" He had the same answer every time…" An educated guess." My dad valued education very highly. He earned a bachelor's degree in Engineering and he studied at OU. I remember bringing all my books home from school to study because I saw how much he valued education. When I was in the 3rd grade I remember coming to class and Mrs. Akard told us to turn in our homework. I did not do my homework, so she gave me a choice of writing 100 times on the board "I will not forget to do my homework" or choose to get a spanking with a paddle. I did not want to be humiliated in front of the entire class, so I chose to get spanked with the paddle instead. I would be up with a flashlight many nights doing my homework after that to spare myself from getting a spanking. Mrs. Akard really cared about me. One day I was acting up in class and she brought me out into the hall, and she asked me what was going on with my behavior. I told her that I was scared that my parents were getting a divorce. I remember my parents getting into arguments and how sad and unstable I would feel when my mom would ask if we wanted to live with her if she left.

My mother was diagnosed with bipolar disorder when I was 22 years old. She would tell us stories of her childhood that were very shocking. My grandmother was 13 years old when she became pregnant and she delivered my mother two months early. My mom said she weighed only two pounds when she was born. My mother was raised by her grandparents and her grandfather was an over-the-road truck driver and her grandmother died when my mother was 6 years old. My mother would tell us stories of other kid's parents not allowing their children to play with mom because of how she dressed and looked at school. She dropped out of school in the 8th grade. She would tell us about her mother's boyfriends touching her inappropriately. It is so hard to imagine how much my mother had to overcome to be the kind of mom she was to us. She was our biggest cheerleader. She loved being our mom and she was a very dedicated mom. I remember there were days that we would leave for school and when we came home, she would still be laying on the couch. She used to tell me, "People are going to think the worst of you no matter what you do." I would internalize those words into my heart and believe them. She would come to all our sporting events and cheer as loudly as she could. When we got older, we started feeling embarrassment and shame from much of my mother's behavior. She was different from the other moms. Instead of being excited about having the loudest cheerleader, our desire to be liked by other people caused us to compare her to the other moms.

When I was around 12 years old, my hands, feet, and underarms would produce large amounts of sweat. I noticed that I was the only person that sweat like I did. I would hide my hands by sticking them in my pockets or under my arms. I would wear clothes that would not show the sweat from my underarms and paid close attention that if anyone did notice that they would not shun me. I was dealing with mass amounts of shame. The shame I felt would lead me to be so self-conscience and disconnected from others. I was so fearful that if anyone really knew that my hands, feet, and underarms sweat as badly as they did, that they would think the worst of me. My brothers, Larry and Tony, and my sister, Tanna, were extremely popular in school and very athletic. Larry, my oldest brother, was exceptionally talented in baseball. He was drafted by the Philadelphia Phillies while playing college baseball. He had a motorcycle accident a few weeks later and was unable to join their baseball team. Tony was an exceptional wrestler and competed at state. Tanna excelled at basketball and played college basketball. The one sport I excelled in was tennis and my friend and I were able to compete at state in doubles. My dad happened to be in town, and he surprised me by coming to see me play and I was so nervous and tense that I played horribly, and we lost our match. I could only feel more shame now because once again, I did not measure up. I would tell myself that I was abandoned for a reason. I would tell myself that my sweating was my fault. I would tell myself that no matter how hard I tried that I would not measure up. The one thing that I could do was to study and try to make good grades. That pleased my dad when I was in the third grade. He noticed me then. He was so proud of me and got me a barbie doll with a house and 2 sets of barbie doll clothes. I remember feeling so good about myself that day. I wanted so badly for my mom and dad to be proud of me.

So many of my thoughts of my childhood have carried into my adulthood. Do you know that God sees vulnerable people? He responds to them. People matter to God. Isaiah 43:2 states" When you go through deep waters, I will be with you. When you go through rivers of difficulty, you will not drown. When you walk through the fire of oppression, you will not be burned up; the flames will not consume you." I believe that we all have a God-shaped hole in our hearts that ONLY God can fill. The longing that I had when I was younger was "Do I matter to my Dad?" "Is my dad proud of me?" I would replay the tapes in my mind of not measuring up. As an adult, I would suffer from major depression 4 times. I have tried neurofeedback which is a way to train brain activity that usually uses EEG data from your brain waves to change your physiological activity. The therapist places scalp sensors on your head to monitor the brain's activity in hopes to train the brain to reach its optimal level. I went faithfully for 5 years to neurofeedback training. I also tried individual counseling for 2 years. I went to celebrate recovery faithfully for 6 months. I completed an online course of cognitive behavioral therapy for 6 months. I also went to several psychiatrists that wanted to just prescribe me meds. I investigated ECT therapy also. Electroconvulsive therapy is a procedure in which electrical currents are passed through the brain that creates a seizure while the patient is under anesthesia. It is intended to relieve the person's depression by changing the brain's chemistry and in turn change how they feel. I researched another form of brain therapy called Transcranial Magnetic Stimulation in which a machine is used to cause an electrical current at a specific area in the brain to stimulate nerve cells in the area of the brain thought to control mood. Over a course of 36 consecutive sessions, it is supposed to lower the symptoms of depression. Going every day and talking with the sweet Christian who would place the machine to my brain actually helped me more than the treatments. I felt so much better and felt like I had hope again. A month afterward my brother, Tony, was driving home in very heavy rain and hydroplaned sideways into another vehicle and he suffered a traumatic brain injury. This event coupled with losing my job would lead me into one of the worst depressions. I am married to the most amazing husband who has been so encouraging and so supportive! I call him "Ivan the great" because he has truly been the kindest to me during all my depression. My son, Joshua, is one of the kindest men you could ever meet and my daughter, Shanna, is one of the most warm-hearted women you could ever meet. I have 3 stepsons that are a joy to hang out with. My Aunts and cousins are one of my greatest blessings and available anytime I call them and are willing to share their experiences in life. I have friends, Pam Lancaster and Denise Drayton, who loved me unconditionally and did not give up on me no matter how much I isolated myself from them. I have an amazing home group from my church, The Village in Flowermound, that has been such a blessing to us. I have a God that chose me when I was young and has been with me all along. Why would I be so depressed when I have so much to be thankful for? I remember having one worry and dwelling on that for days and then I would find another worry and dwell on that for days. I became so anxious that I would just shake because of lack of sleep. I would imagine myself being admitted to a hospital because I could not sleep. I would be so fearful of nighttime coming that my heart would race, and I could not stop worrying. I had already tried so many things. I thought the Lord had this as my plan. My mother had tried to commit suicide twice while living with me at college and I knew that is where I was headed. I fell on my knees and cried out to the Lord "Please help me?!" The Lord hears our cries for help. Psalm 30:2 states "Lord my God, I cried to you for help, and you restored my health. You brought me up from the grave, O Lord. You kept me from falling into the pit of death." I looked up intensive outpatient therapy and the Lord allowed me to go to a Christian- based program that helped to change my life. The program had regular people that were struggling with anxiety and depression just like I was. I had been trying so hard to figure out how to heal my depression and anxiety by myself that I would not dare open up to others for fear of embarrassment that they would judge me so harshly and reject and abandon me. I would hurt so badly that I started planning my own suicide. The psalms in the Bible were what I would turn to just to try to feel close to anyone that had struggled like I did. During my time at the Meier Clinic Catalyst program, one of the assignments was that we were to write our own psalm. This was my psalm to represent my darkest hours of depression.

> *Lord, the pain and suffering I have endured is so tormenting. It stole part of my being. The seconds I counted as I lay awake at night with racing thoughts that forever taunt me! The hell that could never be escaped was so real to me. And who could console me? No one in the entire universe could! I could not bear another day like this! Surely the only way to escape is by taking my life. I would be drawn to Kavorkian if he were ever in my vicinity. I longed for cancer…I longed for a car accident to take my life. I would dream of a quick and painless death. Should I dare take a handful of my Ativan or a handful of my Restoril or better yet my Lunesta and go peacefully in the lake that is so close to my house. I plotted on how to walk there so there is no trace. So, no one has to be embarrassed that I took my own life. I am so done with this life. I called out so many times and there was no reprieve. The Lord had forgotten me. No, He was angry with me. No, He is going to use this death somehow for His glory. The pain, the pain, the pain is too great! Why me? What did I do to deserve such a horrid life? I cannot even show my face because I am so ashamed of all my awful choices that have brought me here.*

This Psalm was exactly how my life had felt. You know what I really needed? I needed hope. I kept praying and asking the Lord to heal me. I could not understand why He would not just make all my pain go away. I was on my hands and knees so many nights begging the Lord to help me. I just wanted the aching in my heart to go away. I just wanted the cloud of sadness to end. The Lord showed me how my thoughts and actions greatly influenced how I felt. Satan came against my thoughts the greatest when I would start worrying. Faith is what pleases God. I prayed so hard, but my feelings and emotions ruled my thoughts. For me to experience the power of God to change my thoughts there had to be all these struggles. I found out from first-hand experience that the Lord would allow ALL my trials to show His healing power and how

He would get the glory from my suffering and adversity. In Isaiah 55:8 it states "My thoughts are nothing like your thoughts, says the Lord. And my ways are far beyond anything you could imagine." We do not think like God. God knew how He would bring me through each time. Galatians 5:5 states "But we who live by the Spirit eagerly wait to receive by faith the righteousness God has promised to us." I just needed to wait in eager anticipation that the Lord had a plan to bring me through each time and closer to Him. That I needed to take my thoughts captive and pay close attention to how I talked to myself and close attention to the fiery darts of worry that Satan was trying to get me to dwell on. Sweet friend.... there is hope! God is our hope! He uses ordinary circumstances to create extraordinary stories in our lives if we will just realize that He is in total control and sovereign.

Sharron Rivera lives in Lake Dallas, Texas and is happily married to her best friend Ivan and is a mother of 2 of her own children and 3 stepchildren. She obtained her bachelor's in accounting and worked as an accountant before going back to school to become a registered nurse. She has a passion to show others that suffer from depression and anxiety that they are loved and valued. She enjoys riding horses, dancing, playing tennis and ping pong. She and her husband have a deep desire to help other married couples that are struggling.

CHAPTER 11

FROM GOD'S GRACE TO GOD'S MERCY

JERRI JERGER VAUGHN

As I began this chapter I began to reminisce and decided to share several nuggets of how God orchestrated throughout my life in different ways. It made me realize we all have to dig ourselves out of the pit we fell into just like in the Bible. We saw Joseph thrown in the pit by his siblings as jealousy set in them. I read in the Bible that in the beginning we were with God and chosen by God. So, to me it was God who put us into the womb of our mother, no matter how we got there.

God had a purpose He created us for. When our family began, we had trust issues. I call the generational curses, abandonment, adultery, rejection and now the curse of divorce started in our family line. I begin to see this all in my mind, as I look back how God orchestrated all along how he was going to use me for. All I can say is, "Why me Lord?"

I will begin my life testimonies with me walking home from school. A lady I did not know asked me if I would sit and talk with her. She told me she wanted me to meet her son, who was coming home from the Army soon. She said I moved here to get my kids in a new environment. She did not like the relationships they had been in.

This man turned out to be the man I married. She had many choices to choose to talk with her, as my sisters and my friends walked that same path. But today, I see the blueprint of why God chose me to be the one who would marry her son and be the one to take care of her kids. But I will always wonder what did God show her about me and why me, Lord! What did I ever do for this to be given to me?

We married and within months, we had miscarried the only little girl we would ever have. Then after 3 years we got the phone call his step dad had died. It was hard on both of us trying to obey his dying mother's only wish to keep the kids together. The kids were 17, 14, 11 and 8, we had a 2-year-old son and I am 8 months pregnant with my second son. We were not prepared for these children after they had been living with an alcoholic dad and now my husband is always gone.

By this time, I am 19 years old and just learning how to be a mom. Yet, in a still small voice, God would always say to me, "Who's going to love them?" Do I run with my own children and break up our family? Can I be submissive when he is just as devastated as I am? I fell to my knees crying behind closed doors as I hid this from my husband and my mother. I felt God said, "Get up and find a home to live in."

I raised the kids alone since my husband decided work was his priority. My husbands' lifestyle began to change and it caused us to lose ourselves and never find us again. All these things that came into our marriage really took us into a life we never knew how to walk through. We never stopped loving each other we just lost how to love each other.

I instead accepted him always working to make ends meet that led to our broken marriage. My husband had to get two jobs to support six children and pay two funeral bills, and it led him to go in paths he said he never wanted to go. He fell into his pit while trying to save us all. We went on to have 2 more sons and I had miscarried another son which was my third son's twin because of the stress of my marriage and the issues I had to cope with.

All my life, family was everything to me. I guess this is why my mom would call me when someone was in need, and I would go. My life was tested like Job and Joseph. I lost everything in the end but my children as God had to separate me from my immediate family to die to my flesh to be used by God. I overcame fear by *Forcing Emotions Away Regardless* in order to build my faith as it *Frees All Inside To Healing*. God allowed all of this for me to become an intercessor.

Forgiveness is a gift to our self, and becomes the opportunity to free oneself and open up inside to a deeper place to grow with God. Before today, my life was always scarred deep in me by abandonment, rejection and now betrayal. I lived with my husband's adultery lifestyle for 32 years with God leading me to stay married saying, "If you don't love him, who will?"

My immediate family damage began with my father too. I want you to step into an experience I had about my father. I can hardly hold back the tears as I remember the day The Holy Spirit had begun to start working on me inside. He told me to go to my dad and tell him that we forgive him. I know God will not always tell you to reconnect, but I believe God was teaching me how to love through Him while answering the heart of two people so far apart.

One day, I was visiting my mom, and my sister had told her what God wanted me to do. My Mom said to me, "Why do you think you have to tell him you forgive him? He needs to tell you to forgive him." Our damage went deeper in my sisters than I have shared but the Bible says to not forgive is a sin. We may not forget, but we have to forgive."

It is the only way for us to be free, otherwise that person holds us captive in our thoughts. My mother never spoke negative of our dad, so I didn't go. I didn't want to do anything to hurt my Mom. It was just something God was showing me to do. to bring healing through me for my dad and maybe for me in some way, too. Looking back, I learned that God knows all things!

I put it aside and went on with life, but it kept bothering me. I don't know why I didn't pick up the phone and just call him in secret. No one would have to know I did it, just to obey God. You will know when God is speaking to you, as it becomes a heaviness you can't shake within you and you will know without a doubt.

A couple of months later, my mother's social security check was bigger, so I called them to see why this happened, and they said my father had died. My heart sank. I had failed God. When I left my Mom's to go home, I was having a hard time with this. I cried, asking God, "How can you forgive me when I didn't obey you to give him the forgiveness he needed before he died?

I'm so sorry his heart did not get to hear he was forgiven. This sick feeling, I felt for not obeying God would not go away, so I drove to the town where he lived and saw a small graveyard next to a church and went in to see if he was buried there. I walked around and actually found his grave. I could only imagine what God's plan was all about.

I really believe The Holy Spirit was guiding me and leading my footsteps, and I sat down on the bench at his grave and I just felt so empty. I wondered if he had gone to church there and maybe gotten saved, and in a few minutes, the Pastor came out of the church, and came over to me and asked me if I knew him. I said, "He was my father; I just never knew him as a dad." We didn't have good memories of him as a dad, so we never tried to be in his life. I cried, telling him that I had failed God when he wanted me to tell him we forgive him and I didn't come. And he said, "I know that was God, because I spent a lot of time with him, and he had gotten saved, but he could never stop crying about what he did to all of you."

We talked awhile, and I left and went and picked up a Belton newspaper and looked up the obituary of his passing. I was reading it, and no one had listed any of us as his children. We were not in his life as his kids while he was alive and now, we were not recognized as his kids in his death. It was sad for me to see that for some reason. In my heart I could not stop crying.

It led me to understand how we commit spiritual adultery. I don't know why it was emotional for me for some reason. I felt God's pain with his children not spending time with him. When we leave God out of our life and get our heart involved with worldly things more than God, we also commit spiritual adultery as we separate from God.

I went on home from my dad's grave and decided to go to Bishop T D Jake's service. I went to get closure so I could get past this. At the end of the service, he called people down front for prayer. I was crying so deep inside me of never having a chance to know what a father was like for a little girl.

And all of a sudden, a piece of paper fell in front of me, and I bent down to pick it up, and I asked several people, "Did you drop this?" No one claimed it. So, I said, "It must be for me," and I turned it over to see what was written, and my heart just broke. It was all the names of my Heavenly Father.

I just broke inside, crying. Thank you, God, for reminding me that you are my father and everything I need you to be. It made me realize I cannot allow anyone to ever stop me from doing whatever God shows me to do. Even if I don't understand something, God will always be true to loving us. I truly believe God was going to do something wonderful with this in my life, and now, I lost that opportunity.

It was just a different feeling for something my life needed, and my Heavenly Father knew all through my life I had something missing. I needed healing of all the missing relatives that I grew up without them in my life. We made our home the gathering place every weekend and most of the holidays. We didn't want our children to grow up without their family like we did.

As we grew up in the right place at the right time, we found a church that worked with Missions even though they divided the wealthy from the poor. They did everything for our church. This is where I learned about God but I did not learn *to know* him. In the summer they sent us to church camp at Mount Lebanon and I asked Jesus to come into my heart at 11 years old.

I had a hard time believing that I am somebody of value when I was young. Rejection can come in all forms of relationships. I know God is a relationship and He longs for us to have one with Him in a real personal way. I never held anything against anyone, because I don't believe they even realized how it made us feel. Jesus said, "Forgive them, for they know not what they do."

I was reading in the bible that in the beginning, God spoke to Adam and Eve what to eat and what not to eat in the garden he created. I saw Satan come along speaking into Eve's ear. As he spoke, he twisted the words God spoke to her and destroyed what God spoke. This just proves we can hear voices inside us saying things to us that was not true. Then, if we allow the voices to manifest, we start to believe them. If we would talk to someone to teach us how to rebuke the devil, we would not be deceived.

Words are powerful but we have to stop the enemy from leading us before we accept the wrong voice. If we hide it, it leads us the wrong way. In my life, all of the trauma I went through was a great lesson. It led me to find God as my Loving Father who was holding me together to bring me to my purpose to mend the brokenhearted. The Holy Spirit taught me to love the unlovable and to forgive the unforgivable was the Agape Love of God He wants his children to walk in.

Today, so many doctrines are teaching what they have chosen for us to know as man's way to God. I only pray I can make a difference in someone's life by sharing how real God can be. God will help us get through all of life's challenges that knock on our door when we return to him. I strongly hear God say, "Who will pay the price to know me?"

I began my walk with God as I stepped out of my doctrine and began to watch Christian TV; I felt something I had not felt before. My heart began to hunger and thirst as I grew to become an intercessor for all my family members. This was something different I had not known about, but through my hunger, I became an intercessor for God as He taught me how to pray for people that needed healing.

I started going to Benny Hinn crusades with an open mind just to observe to see if all this healing was real. Who is this Holy Spirit Benny talks so much about? The more I went the more my faith built. I don't know if it was really doubt that I felt, or as the Bible says, lack of knowledge. My Baptist doctrine had not allowed the Holy Spirit to have his way. I learned the more worship the more real God becomes.

I felt such a difference my family had not experienced in their life as a Christian. I saw more of a law to live the Christian life, because we were taught to obey. I saw being involved in organizations, instead of the Holy Spirit being involved in our lives. There is absolutely no one who could take this new walk with God from me that I had received and experienced for myself and I desired more.

We can read the Bible, go to church, pray, sing in the choir, teach Sunday school, and even preach and not know God. I saw as we worship Jesus, the Holy Spirit reveals the truth as He is called the Anointing and the yokes will be broken out of our life. God removes them as we turn our eyes on Jesus and off of all man. I know this kind of love is not natural to love people that hurt you. I know that God is doing it through me. When we surrender all that we are and have to Him, God is able to take you to a place you have never been. God allowed me to experience how to be in the world, but not of the world. You just kind of feel like you are here, but you feel separate in a spirit world that is not to our understanding.

We know the old you would not be able to handle what you are going through. I would want to leave the alcohol and adultery situation. But I knew that I knew I could not leave when God was using me to teach him real love. As God would pour more love in me for my husband. I would cry many times; God take this cup from me! I heard God whisper, "If you don't love him, who will?

God would bring to my remembrance when Jesus was in Gethsemane and his sweat turned to blood showed me how heavy this cup was for Jesus to carry and to fulfill. Jesus had asked the disciples to pray for him as Jesus cried out "Father, if it be your will take this cup from me." God had sent his son Jesus who had come here to save the world. I realized why my cup had become hard for me when God spoke, he was going to use me for my family members.

Our fleshly desire has to die in order for God to be lifted up. As I turned the flesh off, we call the world, I recovered when I refocused to seek God deeper. Then you have to want God's will for your life more than you want anything else. The day I hungered is the day God began to chisel away all my heartaches created me into a diamond and I was set free.

My husband's mind was messed up from the life style he chose as he gave away our multimillion-dollar company we had been blessed with for 23 years. I learned how God's Love abounds within me as I experienced God's love as I entered into God's Grace to God's Mercy. I began to fully understand how to love through God's Love.

Today, I am a survivor through many challenges in my life. I give thanks to Pastor Benny who taught me strength in my walk with The Holy Spirit and in God's gift of Healing. I was called into the Healing Ministry in many ways as I sat under his Healing Ministry for 10 years volunteering.

I want to thank my 4 sons and 12 grandchildren. When I went through the hardest times in my life you were the glue that held me together. Thank you to my older sons and their wives for the different financial help you gave me and Blake. I want to show my gratitude and appreciation to my youngest son for his strength and walk with God. He was 15 when we lost everything. Instead of becoming angry in his life, he ran to God. He kept me motivated and strong when I lost everything financially overnight. He paid his own way through college with school loans to get his master's and then joined the Navy. He moved me to Hawaii to enjoy my life while he was stationed there. After coming through a near death experience with septic, I needed all the sunshine and love I could get.

I have seen my health change through prayer, and natural supplements, as I heard God speak "Healing is in my Leaves as I learned the fruit and the seed is for healing in the body." If you are looking for a change in life or to contact me my email is:

Jerrivaughn.lovinggodmore@gmail.com

CHAPTER 12

FINDING FREEDOM

MELISSA ROHLFS

Ever wonder how a former sugar addict who had a broken relationship with food became a holistic health and life coach who helps women break free from sugar and stress eating so they can be calm, confident and free? Jesus. He is how.

I'd love to share how finding freedom from food and sugar changed my whole life. In order to understand my transformation, it is important to share with you a little bit of my history. Most of my life was a struggle with low self-worth and self-esteem that resulted in a lack of self-care and emotional eating.

When I was 2 years old my dad passed away unexpectedly. To be clear, my dad was murdered. He didn't die of cancer or in an accident, but he died pretty brutally and it was headline news in my small hometown in Indiana. Growing up, as the only child of a single mom, I turned to food to cope and ease the pain at a very young age. Shortly after his death, my mom started me in dance and I began performing as way of hiding my pain.

When I was six, my mom remarried a man with a child of his own and remember feeling like this was my happy ever after. This new environment created a lot of uneasiness and anxiety, and this is my earliest memory of hiding food in my room for comfort. A furry rodent's feces on the bed tattled on me for keeping a stash of sweets in my room. I continued in dance and did a lot of things to perform and really kind of paint this picture that everything was fine and good. In high school, I developed an eating disorder so that I could be "thin enough" to earn the attention of a boy. Looking back, I believe that was my father wound coming forward and really seeking that affirmation and validation because I didn't receive that from my dad. In high school I was also very active in sports, a class officer, in show choir and dance. It was kind of my way of hiding some of the dysfunction in our family if you will. I graduated from high school and went off to college at Purdue University.

Ironically enough, I had jaw surgery my freshman year at Purdue and I went through sorority rush with my jaw wired shut. Because of that, I was on a liquid diet for four weeks and lost quite a bit of weight. So, I went through sorority rush and was accepted into the Delta Gamma house. I really had a beautiful college experience, however, my unhealthy eating patterns continued. I would overeat. I would under eat. I would hide food in my room and eat my roommate's chocolates. One healthy habit I developed in college was I learned to exercise on a regular basis for stress management. I also continued to do "all of the things" in college. I was an officer in my sorority house, involved in Panhellenic Council, InterVarsity Christian Fellowship, Purdue Musical Organizations, and much more. I was really burning myself out and would turn to food for comfort. During my time at Purdue, I began my relationship with Jesus. I did grow up going to church, but didn't know that Jesus wanted a relationship with me until learning this truth in college. It was a life changing moment for sure!

After graduating from college, I got a great job in downtown Chicago was super excited to be working in the big city! Food really was my comfort, as I turned to the deep-dish pizza, and ice cream if I had had a bad day. I was only in Chicago for a short while because after a year, I was called on to InterVarsity Christian Fellowship staff in Madison, Wisconsin.

Shortly after I moved to Wisconsin, I met my husband at church. We got married and five years later, we had our daughter. This is really kind of when my healing journey began. When our daughter was three months old, we had friends from church over for a Fourth of July party. I remember she was just crying unconsolably and I didn't know what to do. I felt very overwhelmed in that moment and a friend suggested going to a chiropractor. I thought "why would we take a newborn baby to the chiropractor, you are crazy." But being a new, overwhelmed mom and kind of at my wit's end, we decided to give it a try and it was so life-changing for us. It was at that chiropractic appointment that we learned our daughter had an issue with dairy. With me nursing her, I cut dairy out of my diet and her colic got a little bit better. The chiropractor also suggested craniosacral therapy since she was born via c-section. So, we did chiropractic, craniosacral therapy, and I cut out dairy and her colic got so much better. I was so thankful and I think for the first time, my eyes were opened to alternative ways of doing things when it came to health.

I remember taking our daughter to our pediatrician and the pediatrician said "it's colic, all babies have it and she'll outgrow it." That was just such an unacceptable answer to me. If my child is crying, I want to know why my baby is crying and what I can do to help her. I'm not willing to accept that it could just be what babies do. That did not work for me, so I think that helped me to be open to the chiropractic experience. It was a life changer and step one on the journey to holistic health.

Shortly after starting chiropractic care, we moved to Illinois and not long afterwards, we had our son. I was completely overwhelmed at this point. My husband was traveling for work at the time, our daughter was now 27 months old, and on top of this, I had this newborn baby who wasn't sleeping. We were also attempting to potty train our daughter who had undiagnosed food allergies and some sensory challenges. I had no clue what to do or how to handle this exhaustion and my feelings. I remember eating Oreo cookies in the pantry because I was just so overwhelmed. One day, we took our son to the chiropractor because he was fussy and the chiropractor asked me what I had eaten. I told her some Oreos. Then she asked "how many." And, I had to tell her I had eaten the whole package because I was so overwhelmed. She gently and lovingly explained that you know this isn't the best for you or the baby. I know that you're overwhelmed but let's figure out a way to maybe take care of that without food and that was another pivotal moment in my journey.

Right around that time as well, I had started a professional women's networking group. There were so many great women involved and it was a really a life-giving experience for me. A life coach joined this group and with me being hungry for growth and change, this seemed like a great opportunity for me. As I was feeling a little bit stuck in motherhood, I decided to meet with this life coach to figure out my purpose in the world beyond parenting. God must want more for me than staying home with this baby who wasn't sleeping and a child who was fussy, right?

I started to regularly meet with my life coach, who also happened to be a licensed therapist, and she diagnosed me with PTSD as a result of trauma that had occurred in my childhood. This also explained why I was turning to food so often as a child. Because of my PTSD diagnosis, I tried Prozac and it didn't work. Actually, it made things worse for me. I know everybody's different and we need to do what is best for us, so I went to a holistic doctor to explore my options. Her first step was to test the levels of vitamins and minerals in my body. We ran urine tests, saliva tests, and blood draws, and ultimately discovered that I was severely nutrient deficient, and she encouraged me to start a variety of supplements. At this point I was living off of Diet Dr Pepper, sugar, and carbohydrates. I was crying in the bathroom because I was overwhelmed. I was hiding in the pantry to eat. I was not in a good place physically, mentally or emotionally. She started me on a regimen of supplements which worked very well. During this time, we were actively involved in our church. We attended a weekly small group and I frequently visited the intercessory healing prayer room. I believe this is how God answered my prayers, through His power and using the holistic doctor and therapist. This church was a major part in my faith journey as my eyes were open to the power of the Holy Spirit and His role in our lives.

Not long after this, we moved to South Dakota so my husband could have a job that did not require travel. While we were there, I joined a gym, because our kids could be in childcare, I could work out, drink a latte at the cafe and have some space to myself. I attended a jazzercise class and it was so fun! I was starting to make relationships with women in the class and I was sharing with some of them that I was eating thin mints in the pantry. At this point, one woman said, "Well why were you eating them in the pantry? Were you hiding?" At that point, it was kind of like a light bulb went off. There might be a pattern here. Why do I hide when I eat the treats? This started in my childhood.

Around this time we also discovered our daughter was intolerant to not only dairy, but also wheat. Since my child had food intolerances, I thought that based on my history, allergy testing might be helpful for me as well. Testing confirmed that I also had the same food intolerances. Isn't God gracious to lead us gently, one step at a time? With us moving to South Dakota, we joined a church there and God really connected us with an amazing couple. I had been praying for a mentor since becoming a mother and feel like this couple was such an answer to prayer! They walked us through deliverance and journeyed with us through some inner healing. Jesus really used them to help us to break free from some strongholds that were in our past weighing us down. My shackles of low self-worth, low self-esteem, and not feeling good enough were removed as part of the deliverance process.

It was right around this time when I was introduced to the concept of whole foods and eating foods in their most natural form. As I eliminated the foods that I was intolerant to from my diet and began to eat nutritious whole foods, I implemented daily exercise and I finally started to break free from sugar. I felt alive and amazing! Not only was I spiritually free from past wounds, for the first time in my journey I became physically free from sugar addiction.

As the Lord healed my inside and set me free, a transformation occurred on the outside as well. The inner healing, the mindset work and changing my diet led to quite a physical transformation that others could see. Realizing my self-worth, that I mattered and was worth taking care of, combined with the dietary changes, led people to see the change and ask what I was doing. Because of my journey, I felt called to help others who are where I was. For me, it wasn't about weight. I think people saw me and they saw the weight loss and physical change, but I knew there was freedom from anxiety, stress, chaos, and confusion. I had a clear brain, energy and a zest for life, instead of being lethargic and in a fog. Jesus transformed and healed my relationship with sugar and food to bring peace to my life. He has made me calm and confident and free in HIM. This, in turn, makes me free around food, sugar and what I used to turn to in order to escape, numb or soothe. This healing journey has transformed how I see food and I now understand its impact on all areas of health ~ not just weight.

Because of my journey, I went to school because I really wanted to help other women learn how to change their habits, their thoughts and their relationship with food, and ultimately themselves. Women can be free when they see themselves as Daughters of the King and live in that freedom, He gave us.

I have learned it's not about meal plans or calorie counting. It's not about the things we turn to. It's really about your relationship with yourself, learning to listen to your body, and your relationship with food. It's about seeing yourself and treating yourself as a Daughter of The King. He showed me the power of food and the impact it has on all areas of health. So many times, we just associate it with weight, when really, He created us as whole creatures and desires to treat the whole person, holistically! Realizing the impact of food on my life {beyond weight} and transforming my mind, empowered me to change my habits. It made me realize how food made me FEEL and some foods aren't worth eating if they don't make you feel good and energetic! Thankfully He broke those chains and sugar no longer controls me like it used to.

I am calm, confident, and empowered to be all God made me to be! I'm strong because of His healing work in me. I realize I live for Him alone and what other people think of me doesn't matter. That is significant freedom for me as a recovering people pleaser {and another thing I used sugar to self soothe!} When you get to the root of the issue, that is where healing begins.

Quick fixes deceive us. So many times, we try to treat a problem with a band-aid instead of healing the root cause. If we take time to step back and look at the big picture, the root can be addressed and lasting transformation can occur. In John 5, Jesus asks the man at the pool if he wants to be well. The man says yes. Jesus replies, "Get up! Pick up your mat and walk." {v.8} The biggest take away from my journey is a lot of times we need to not only pray, but also take action. Much like the man at the pool, we need to pick up our mats and walk. Your freedom is waiting sweet sister. Go grab it!

Melissa Rohlfs is a certified holistic health and life coach helping busy women break free from sugar and stress/emotional eating so they can be calm, confident and in control. Around food. Around sugar. In stressful situations. In their bodies. In their life. She is committed to empowering women to break free from dieting, emotional eating and self-image issues so they can ditch the diet mentality, and feel empowered in their own skin and be free to be who God made them to be. After her own tumultuous history with food {withholding and then later in life, bingeing}, she learned how to deal with the core issues around her broken relationship with food. As a result, she felt called to go to school and learn to teach other women how to do the same. She graduated from the Health Coach Institute as a Holistic Health and Life Coach in 2018 and is the proud owner of Free 2 B Coaching. She is a proud Boilermaker alumna living in Tucson with her husband, Chad and two kiddos.

Links:
www.free2bcoaching.com
www.facebook.com/MelissaRohlfsCoach
https://www.instagram.com/free2b_coaching/
Podcast ~ https://anchor.fm/melissa-rohlfs

www.ingramcontent.com/pod-product-compliance
Lightning Source LLC
LaVergne TN
LVHW011728060526
838200LV00051B/3075